MW01630894

THE FIRST AMERICAN FLAG

Revisiting the Grand Union at Prospect Hill

BYRON DE LEAR

The Flag Research Center

Studies in Flag History and Symbolism

Other Works in this Series

Canada's Flag: A Search for a Country
John Ross Matheson

A History of Irish Flags From Earliest Times
Gerard Anthony Hayes-McCoy

Studies in Flag History and Symbolism

THE FIRST AMERICAN FLAG

Revisiting the Grand Union at Prospect Hill

Byron DeLear

Edgehill Books
Austin

EDGEHILL BOOKS
Austin, Texas

"All ye inhabitants of the world, and dwellers on the earth, see ye, when he lifteth up an ensign on the mountains; and when he bloweth a trumpet, hear ye." ISAIAH 18:3

Edgehill Books is a trademark of Talbot Publishers, Ltd. Co.

TALBOT PUBLISHERS

Published in the United States
by Talbot Publishers, Ltd. Co.

Publisher's Cataloging-in-Publication Data
Names: DeLear, Byron, author.
Title: The First American Flag: Revisiting the Grand Union at Prospect Hill / Byron DeLear.

Series: Studies in Flag History and Symbolism

Description: Includes bibliographical references and index. | Austin, TX: Talbot Publishers, Ltd. Co., 2018.

Identifiers: ISBN 978-1-946831-01-9 (Hardcover) | 978-1-946831-02-6 (pbk.)
Subjects: LCSH United States—History—Revolution, 1775-1783—Flags. | Flags—United States—History–18th century. | Boston (Mass.)—History–Revolution, 1775-1783. | BISAC HISTORY / United States / Revolutionary Period (1775-1800) | SOCIAL SCIENCE / Customs & Traditions | REFERENCE / Signs & Symbols

Classification: LCC CR113 .D45 2017 | DDC 929.9/20973—dc23

ISBN 978-1-946831-01-9 (Hardcover) |
978-1-946831-02-6 (pbk.)
Printed in the United States

Dedication

To my loving mother, Wilma Ruth De Lear: "You have it to do."

To my father, Walter Walker De Lear, a patriot with an ethos: "Patience and quality."

To my wife, my soulmate, Vicki Lorenz Englund.

Wynkoop Motto:
Virtutem Hilaritate Colere
"To adorn excellence with joyousness"

Contents

Foreword

With this work, the Flag Research Center resumes publication of its monograph series, *Studies in Flag History and Symbolism*. This series fills a deep void in the humanities and social science literature by focusing on monograph-length works that both critically examine and deeply explore the usage of flags in political, social, cultural, and historical contexts.

Studies in Flag History and Symbolism was conceived by Whitney Smith in the late 1970s, and two books were published under its aegis: *A History of Irish Flags from Earliest Times* by Gerard Anthony Hayes-McCoy in 1979 and *Canada's Flag* by John Ross Matheson in 1980. As the only professional vexillologist in the United States at the time, Smith was long on ideas and short on money and staff; as his attentions were demanded elsewhere—primarily by the Flag Research Center's consulting practice—the series practically died a-bornin' as no more titles were issued under the series banner (pun intended).

The contributions by Hayes-McCoy and Matheson, however, stand as an example of the value of this series. Thoughtful, well-researched, and a decided point of view were the hallmarks of their works. Hayes-McCoy sought to illuminate the long history of Irish flags overlooked by British authors, who dominated vexillological scholarship throughout most of the 20th century. Matheson provided a unique perspective on the Canadian flag debate of the mid-1960s which resulted in the successful adoption of a new national flag that was not spurred by a fight for independence.

As we enter the post-Whitney Smith period of vexillology, this series is needed now more than ever. The struggles for control of the symbols embodied by a flag continue unabated in the 21st century. Fundamentally, vexillology is about "getting at the processes, roles, and functions of nationalism and patriotism in past or present societies," Dr. Scot Guenter succinctly wrote, "by uncovering and revealing deeper understanding of the range of influences and representations flags can provide as symbols." This work stands in stark contrast to the work of most individuals interested in flags, who obsess over official specifications of flags and other formal characteristics that are almost divorced from the scholarly inquiry described by Dr. Guenter.

Byron DeLear's work stands in the tradition of the earlier contributions to this series. He takes a critical look at the debate surrounding the first American flag—that is, the first flag of an America seeking independence from Great Britain—raised on Prospect Hill. The flag's design is contested among vexillologists, and DeLear seriously examines those contestations. For Americans and their civil religion oriented around their flag, the design of that first American flag is important because the correct historical narrative either reinforces their traditional views of the nature of American independence or undermines those views with one that is less compelling, and thus, less satisfying.

I hope you enjoy reading this gratifying work as much as I did.

Hugh L. Brady
The University of Texas

Austin, Texas
March 2018

Introduction

THE FIRST AMERICAN FLAG is the origin story of a treasured national icon—the Grand Union flag—and examines a critical period at the end of 1775 and beginning of 1776 when several matters of American national identity were established. Considered to be the first American flag, the Grand Union flag was first flown over an inaugural ceremony for the American Navy's first flagship, the *Alfred*, in December 1775 in Philadelphia; and less than a month later, in another military ceremony commemorating the "New Establishment" of the Continental Army. At the dawning of what would become known as America's "Revolutionary Year," the Grand Union was raised on New Year's Day, 1776, on a fortified high-ground overlooking Boston known as Prospect Hill. The very next day, the words "United States of America," were written for the first time in General Washington's Cambridge Headquarters, what is today known as Longfellow House.

Recent research has questioned whether the Grand Union flag, also known as the "Continental Colors," really flew at Boston's Prospect Hill on 1 January 1776. Eyewitness accounts use the term "union flag" and a new interpretation theorizes this to have referred specifically to the British Union Jack and not the characteristic "union flag with 13 red-and-white stripes." This book rebuts the new interpretation and supports the conventional history through an examination of eighteenth-century linguistic standards, contextual historical trends, and additional primary and secondary sources.

Figure 1. *Grand Union flag at top of Prospect Hill in Somerville, MA on 4 March 2018.* Jeanine Farley

THE FIRST AMERICAN FLAG explores this important national icon and how the introduction of this galvanizing symbol occurred at a time when the trappings of American nationhood were taking shape—in less than a month's time, a new navy, a new army, a new flag, and a new name for a nation came into being.

The First American Flag

New Year's Day in Boston can be a frigid affair, but on 1 January 2011 the weather was a balmy (by New England standards) 47 degrees. In the small Boston suburb of Somerville, I was standing with a film crew in the light, slushy snow on Prospect Hill, where locals gathered to witness an annual commemorative event: the unfurling of the "first flag of America"—the Grand Union flag (FIGURES 2 AND 3).

A man on horseback costumed as General George Washington made a speech while the distinctive banner was hoisted to top Prospect Hill's castle-like monument. The long-serving mayor of Somerville, Joseph Curtatone, along with several community leaders and local historians, addressed the crowd. Revolutionary War re-enactors fired a few flintlock volleys to a rousing (and historically accurate) "hip, hip, huzzah!" Patriotic songs were sung, hot cider served, and a few snowballs flew through the air. Our film crew captured it all—along with several man-on-the-street type interviews with re-enactors, historians, and serendipitously, the founder of modern vexillology, Dr. Whitney Smith.

Figure 2. *Revolutionary War re-enactors stand at attention during the Prospect Hill flag-raising ceremony in Somerville, Massachusetts, on 1 January 2011. The annual event commemorates General George Washington's unfurling of the "first flag of America," known as the Grand Union flag, at the dawning of America's Revolutionary Year.* Dave Rutherford, courtesy of House of Motion.

Whitney and I discussed Peter Ansoff's 2006 paper which "present[ed] a hypothesis that the flag raised on Prospect Hill on that historic day was not, in fact, the so-called 'Grand Union,' but simply a British Union flag." I was familiar with Ansoff's well-researched article and had even read online that Smith considered its arguments persuasive. We briefly discussed another running hypothesis about the Grand Union flag; namely, its nearly identical resemblance to the British East India Company flag—a design pre-dating Prospect Hill by over a century.[1] While there is no "smoking gun" evidence of the Grand Union flag ever being connected to, or even influenced by, the East India Company colors, it is important to note that history has yet to discover *any* primary source documents relating to the provenance of the Grand Union flag. Its origin is shrouded in mystery as there is simply no historical record of when—or more importantly why—the Grand Union flag's particular design was proposed and adopted. Why no record has been found could be due to specific documents that are missing which may have plausibly contained the Grand Union flag's origin story. In addition to undiscovered and/or destroyed secret proceedings of Congress, there are missing George Washington letters and papers, most notably from his secretary Lt. Col. Joseph Reed, for the period surrounding Prospect Hill. Reed was the recipient of George Washington's 4 January account of the flag-raising at Prospect Hill (one of three primary source eyewitness accounts of the event) and is the author of one of the only existing flag directives of the immediate period in question.[2] And yet—despite the missing history—we know that in a relatively uniform manner, starting in December 1775, the Grand Union became the de facto standard of the American colonies, and following the Declaration of Independence in July 1776, the "Union Flag of the American States."

Figure 3. *Illustration of the Grand Union flag featuring the British Union Jack and thirteen red and white stripes symbolizing the union of the American colonies. Considered the "first flag of America," the Grand Union was first displayed on the Continental Navy's flagship,* Alfred, *on 3 December 1775 and was in use until late 1777.* Courtesy of Duane Streufert for USFlagDepot.com

Ansoff's paper asserts that no striped union flag flew at Prospect Hill, but rather only a British Union Jack (FIGURE 4). Being that both flags have a British Union in their design, the distinguishing characteristic between the two would be the horizontal red-and-white stripes. Ansoff's theory rests primarily on two legs: (1) In the years leading up to the revolutionary era, English colonists flew British Union Jacks in an *ad hoc* manner with words like "Liberty" emblazoned on them as a "symbol of united resistance to British policies"; and (2) George Washington and other eyewitnesses used the term "union flag" to describe the events that had transpired on Prospect Hill, New Year's Day, 1776.

In rebutting this modern interpretation, I examine the historical record and show through primary source material that it was entirely appropriate for Prospect Hill eyewitnesses to have referred to the Grand Union flag as a "union flag," and the escalating war, late date, and other catalyzing events leading to independence make it highly unlikely for the British Union Jack to have been utilized in an official capacity inaugurating the Continental Army's new establishment.

One eyewitness to the event, for example, mentions the "striped continental" being flown that day, and although somewhat confusing in either describing one or two flags, the bottom line is, stripes still flew at Prospect Hill. Further, secondary accounts report the striped flag at Prospect Hill and are supported by its coinciding and widespread adoption throughout the revolutionary enterprise. If these secondary reports were erroneous, as Ansoff suggests, nowhere were they corrected.

Figure 4. *A British Union Jack, or "King's Colours," displayed by Revolutionary War re-enactors at Fort Ontario on Flag Day, 14 June 2013. This variation of the British Union flag was in use from 1606 to 1801 and featured the intersecting crosses of St. George and St. Andrew representing England and Scotland.* Steve Yablonski, OswegoCountyToday.com

Revising history without clear and unambiguous primary source interpretation should not be taken lightly. With the fact that an eyewitness mentions the "striped continental" at Prospect Hill and numerous other contemporary accounts refer to the new striped flag as a "union flag," a competing hypothesis to Ansoff emerges, one which affirms the traditional history.

Figure 5. Illustration from 1920 by Harry W. Carpenter depicting the Alfred, *the first flagship of the Continental Navy. Formerly a merchant ship named the* Black Prince, *the Congressional Naval Committee purchased the vessel on 4 November 1775 and fitted her out as a man-of-war. The* Alfred *mounted thirty cannon—ten six-pound guns on her main deck and twenty nine-pounders below—and four small swivel guns in her tops. During her commissioning in Philadelphia on 3 December 1775, Lieutenant John Paul Jones hoisted the "Grand Union" flag for the first time.* National Archives and Records Administration.

Although there are many tales and myths about the Grand Union flag's beginnings, the primary source evidence starts with the outfitting of the Continental Navy in Philadelphia. The first public display of the Grand Union flag—or what John Paul Jones calls the "Flag of America"—occurred less than a month before its unveiling on Prospect Hill, and the historical context of these two events make them intrinsically connected (Figure 5).[3] To wit, the former essentially inaugurates a new navy, the latter a new army. Also known as the Continental Colors, Continental Union Flag, First Navy Ensign, Cambridge Flag, or just Union Flag (and many others), for purposes of simplicity this book will utilize its most common appellation: Grand Union flag.

---

[1] Sir Charles Fawcett, "The Striped Flag of the East India Company, and its Connexion with the American Stars and Stripes," *The Journal of the Society for Nautical Research 23* (October 1937), passim.

[2] Adding to the mystery, Reed wrote to John Paul Jones on 20 October 1775 to recommend the Pine Tree Flag—a month-and-a-half before John Paul Jones unveiled the Grand Union on the Continental Navy's flagship *Alfred*. Colonels Glover and Moylan replied the following day: "That as Broughton and Selman, who sailed that morning, had none but their old colors, they had appointed the signal by which they could be known by their friends to be 'the ensign up to

the maintopping lift.'" It may be surmised that by "old colors," they meant either the British Red Ensign or British Union Jack.

[3] Beginning in 1779, there are several statements made by John Paul Jones laying stake to the claim of hoisting the "Flag of Freedom" or "Flag of America" for the first time in December 1775 on the Continental Navy's first flagship *Alfred*. In his letter to Robert Morris dated 10 October 1783, Jones states: "It was my fortune as the senior first lieutenant to hoist the flag of America the first time it was displayed." Of note, Morris was the sole naval agent for much of the Revolutionary War serving on the Naval or Marine Committee, the former owner of the Continental Navy's flagship *Alfred* (as partner in Willing, Morris & Co.), and proprietor of the staging area where the embryonic navy was outfitted. Further, Morris was one of Jones's chief advocates, and eventually, the executor of his will. Considering his audience, it is highly unlikely that Jones would attempt to spin this account too wildly in a self-serving manner, as some historians have suggested. In his letter to Morris, Jones concludes—perhaps in an attempt to temper the braggadocio—"Though this was but a slight circumstance [raising the "flag of America" for the first time], yet I feel for its honor more than I think I should have done if it had not happened." When Jones relayed the same story in letters to Samuel Huttington (President of Congress, 7 December 1779), Baron Van Der Capellen (Dutch Colonel), and the King of France, he does not make light of the event, but rather fully basks in its glory.

The History—Setting the Stage

Following the bloodshed of Lexington and Concord (in April 1775) and the Battle of Bunker Hill (in June 1775), "the British North American colonies from Maine to Georgia were in open rebellion."[4] John Adams wrote in May 1775 that "[t]he martial spirit throughout this province is astonishing. It arose all of a sudden, since the news of the battle of Lexington." The everyday citizen's new mindset was also shared by the Continental Congress, which began necessary preparations for making war against the greatest military power in the world. "Despite lack of international legal recognition," historian Kevin Philips summarizes, "the Continental Congress functioned as a de facto war government. By the end of 1775, the United Colonies had also created an army (June 14), a navy (October 13), and even a marine corps (November 10)."[5]

Figure 6. *USS* Alfred *(formerly,* Black Prince*) pictured in Philadelphia.* Courtesy of the Cochrane Collection, Navy Art Collection, Naval History and Heritage Command.

The first ship to be commissioned by the Continental Navy was the *Black Prince*, a merchant vessel built in 1774 (Figure 6). It was owned by Willing, Morris & Co., a partnership between two of the most successful businessmen in North America, Thomas Willing and Robert Morris, "the financier of the American Revolution."[6] The *Black Prince* was renamed the *Alfred*, according to Adams, "in honor of the founder of the greatest Navy that ever existed."[7] Congress ordered the *Black Prince* to be fitted out as a man-of-war on 30 October 1775.[8] The Continental Navy's first flagship, mounting 30 guns, was publicly reported as "finished" on 18 November.[9]

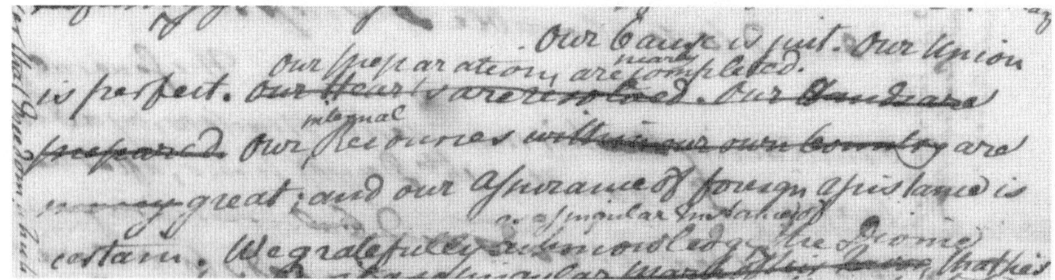

Figure 7. *Detail of John Dickinson's draft copy of the* Declaration of the Causes and Necessity for Taking Up Arms *which was issued by the Second Continental Congress on 6 July 1775. Note the phrase: "Our cause is just. Our union is perfect. Our preparations are nearly completed. Our internal Resources are great; and our assurance [sic] of foreign assistance is certain." The final version deleted: "Our preparations are nearly completed."* Collection of the New York Historical Society.

Four months earlier, the Continental Congress had dispatched its "Olive Branch Petition," an entreaty to England in an attempt to resolve the conflict; yet, simultaneously, in its "Declaration of the Causes and Necessity of Taking Up Arms," they laid before the "opinion of mankind…the justice of our cause," by framing the escalating conflict as an existential dichotomy—either "slavery" at the hands of an overzealous parliament, "or resistance by force."

The document's authors, Thomas Jefferson and John Dickinson, were unambiguous as to which path the United Colonies would take: "The latter is our choice. We have counted this contest, and find nothing so dreadful as voluntary slavery."[10]

Both the Petition and Declaration effectively neutralized one another despite the Crown refusing to receive the peace petition.[11] The Declaration's tone was defiant and would suggest a casting of the die, so to speak: "Our cause is just. Our union is perfect. Our internal resources are great, and, if necessary, foreign assistance is undoubtedly attainable" (Figure 7).

The Petition, primarily made to mollify moderates within Congress, seems totally contradictory (at first-blush) when juxtaposed with the Declaration—but like the Grand Union flag itself, incorporating both British and American elements—these incongruous characteristics together are representative of the transitional nature of the nation-building series of events taking place. The unorthodox nature of what was transpiring during "the fifteen months between the shots fired at Lexington and Concord in April of 1775 and the adoption of the Declaration of

Independence in July of 1776 can justifiably claim to be both the most consequential and...*strangest* year in American history."[12]

Nations and governments are not easily born, and whether steps like the Petition were sincere or merely delaying actions we will never precisely know. There is evidence that supports both contentions. A British informer in Philadelphia commented on Benjamin Franklin's behind-the-scenes attitude toward the conflict suggesting a type of Fabian strategy: "Mr Franklin I find to be a daring arteful insinuating incendeary: The doctrine he Preaches privately is, that if Ammerica can hold out for two years, they may have any term's they require."[13]

Franklin's prognostication may have been a few years short, but ultimately, the war of attrition, both politically and militarily, is what proved to be successful, with, of course, Washington assuming the role of "American Fabius."[14] Perhaps devices such as the Grand Union flag and the Olive Branch were a form of "hedged bet" against the deadly consequences of treason should the revolutionary enterprise fail. If so, this could possibly explain the absence of historical detail—it was left out on purpose.

Despite the Olive Branch Petition and other unsuccessful attempts to resolve the conflict, all-out war was fast approaching. After rebuffing the petition, "On August 23, the King issued a proclamation that said the Americans had 'proceeded to open and avowed rebellion.'"[15]

Indeed, since open hostilities had broken out, positions on both sides had calcified. The Royal Navy's commander of the North American Station, Admiral Samuel Graves, reflected this dangerous polarization in an opinion rendered after Lexington and Concord: "We ought to act hostilely from this time forward by burning and laying waste the whole country."[16]

Throughout the autumn of 1775, war preparations accelerated as the Continental Congress worked feverishly in the midst of an expanding conflict. A British spy wrote to London on 11 September, "military preparations still go's on with unceasing diligence."[17] Secret proceedings had taken place both in the provincial assemblies and Congress to procure that most necessary substance for making war: gunpowder. George Washington's army besieging the British troops in Boston was in dire need of it. Their shortage was so desperate, orders were actually given to use wooden harpoons instead of guns.[18] Merchants, like Robert Morris, "employed every form of subterfuge" in order to smuggle the war materiel into the colonies. By late summer and early autumn, shipments of tons of powder began coming in from around the world. The cost of these initial procurements easily exceeded £100,000, a massive fortune worth approximately $16 million in today's currency (FIGURE 8).[19]

Figure 8. *Philadelphia merchant Robert Morris, "the financier of the American Revolution," was one of only two men to sign the* Declaration of Independence, *the* Articles of Confederation, *and the* Constitution. *He served with Benjamin Franklin on both secret committees of Congress and marshaled his international trading network to supply the Continental Army and Navy with gunpowder and other necessities.* Painting by Charles Willson Peale, Library of Congress Prints and Photographs Division, http://hdl.loc.gov/loc.pnp/cph.3a07081.

On 18 October 1775 the Royal Navy burned the town of Falmouth (modern day Portland, Maine) in a campaign that by New Year's Day had "bombarded, torched, or attempted to burn over a dozen American cities." British General William Howe, writing to Lord Dartmouth, dispassionately reported the results of the attack on Falmouth, which was "destroyed on the 18th of October, burning about five hundred houses, fourteen sea vessels, taking and destroying several others, without any loss on our part."[20] To George Washington, "the burning of Falmouth was 'an outrage exceeding in Barbarity and cruelty every hostile Act practiced among Civilized nations.'"[21]

On 2 December 1775, the day before the Grand Union's debut, the Congress furthered its policy of open-war against the British. It ordered Colonel Benjamin Harrison "to proceed immediately to cruise on, take or destroy as many of the armed vessels, cutters, and ships of war of the enemy as possible" and directed the Naval Committee to prepare "a proper commission for the Captains or Commanders of the ships of war in the service of the United Colonies."[22] Three hundred blank commission forms were ordered that day to be "immediately printed" and orders were given to the colonel of the Pennsylvania Battalion to send a detachment to keep "a regular guard on the wharves of Messrs. Willing and Morris...to take care of the ships and stores belonging to the United Colonies."[23] Prisoners of war were to be treated as such, "but with humanity," and that an exchange of prisoners should be "citizens for citizens, officers for officers of equal rank, and soldier for soldier." The prior resolutions Congress had passed with respect to the "establishment of the new army" (the Army of '76), were ordered to be sent to General Washington in Cambridge "by express."

---

[4] E. Gordon Bowen-Hassell, Dennis M. Conrad, and Mark L. Hayes, *Sea Raiders of the American Revolution: The Continental Navy in European Waters* (Washington, D.C.: Department of Defense, Naval Historical Center, 2003), viii.

[5] Kevin Phillips, *1775: A Good Year for Revolution* (New York: Penguin Group, 2012), 19.

[6] Charles Rappleye, *Robert Morris: Financier of the American Revolution* (New York: Simon & Schuster, 2010), passim. According to Rappleye, Morris founded the first bank in America in order to support his operations as the financier of the American government, established the idea of free capital markets as fundamental to American liberty, and is the architect of the American financial system.

[7] "Diary and Autobiography of John Adams, Philadelphia, December 6, 1775," reprinted in *Naval Documents of the American Revolution* [hereafter *NDAR*], Volume 2, ed. William Bell Clark (Washington, D.C.: Government Printing Office, 1966), 1305. It is notable that the day after the name of the Continental Navy's first flagship was announced (*Alfred*, 17 November 1775), *The Pennsylvania Evening Post* published an extract from *Entick's Naval History* depicting the Anglo-Saxon King Alfred as the "innovator of a new naval order." John J. McCuster, *Alfred: The First Continental Flagship 1775–1778* (Washington D.C.: Smithsonian Institution Press, 1973), 3.

[8] "Journal of the Continental Congress, 30 October 1775," reprinted in *NDAR*, Volume 2, 647.

[9] "Extract of a letter from Philadelphia, Dated Nov. 18," *Dunlap's Maryland Gazette* (Baltimore, 21 November 1775), reprinted in *NDAR*, Volume 2, 1068.

[10] The "Olive Branch Petition" was passed by Congress in July 1775 attempting to stave off total war. "The Declaration of the Causes and Necessity of Taking Up Arms" was also passed in July 1775 and was written chiefly by Thomas Jefferson and John Dickinson.

[11] Pauline Maier, *American Scripture: Making of the Declaration of Independence* (New York: Random House, 1997), passim.

[12] Joseph J. Ellis, *American Creation: Triumphs and Tragedies in the Founding of the Republic* (New York: Alfred A. Knopf/Random House, 2007), 20 (emphasis added by the author).

[13] Geoffrey Seed, "A British Spy in Philadelphia," *The Pennsylvania Magazine of History and Biography* (January 1961), 19.

[14] George Washington was often called the "American Fabius" honoring him with the memory of Quintus Fabius Maximus (c.274–203 BCE), a Roman politician and general known for his delaying military tactics in facing a superior armed force in the Second Punic War. For this reason Fabius Maximus is sometimes considered the "father of guerilla warfare."

[15] Maier, *American Scripture*, passim.

[16] Allen French, *The First Year of the American Revolution* (Boston, Mass.: Houghton Mifflin, 1934), 20.

[17] Gilbert Barkly to Sir Grey Cooper, Philadelphia, 11 September 1775, cited in *Seed*, "A British Spy in Philadelphia," 19.

[18] David McCullough, 1776: "*Orders from Nathanial Greene...*" (New York: Simon & Schuster, 2005), 60.

[19] Charles Rappleye, *Robert Morris: Financier of the American Revolution* (New York: Simon & Schuster, 2010), 36. In the summer and autumn of 1775, provincial Committees of Safety and the Continental Congress began accelerating their pursuit of gunpowder, supplies, and armaments, with Philadelphia merchant Robert Morris playing a pivotal role: "In September, the Congress called on Morris himself, and advanced him a total of eighty thousand pounds to obtain powder in Europe. It was by far the largest munitions contract Congress had yet made." (Rappleye, *Robert Morris*, 36–37.) *In Peter Force's American Archives*, there are numerous other accounts of additional material procurement during the summer and autumn of 1775.

[20] "Letter from General Howe to the Earl of Dartmouth, Nov. 27, 1775," reprinted in Peter Force (comp.), *American Archives*, Series 4, Volume 3 (Washington, D.C.: n.p., 1837–1853), 1678.

[21] Kevin Phillips, *1775: A Good Year for Revolution* (New York: Penguin Group, 2012), 343.

[22] "Journal of the Continental Congress, December 2, 1776," reprinted in *NDAR*, Volume 2, 1231–1232.

[23] Ibid.

The Grand Union Debut

On 3 December 1775, in Philadelphia, First Lieutenant John Paul Jones hoisted the Grand Union flag on the *Alfred*, marking its first documented appearance (Figure 9). Jones later used the terms "Flag of Freedom" or "Flag of America" to describe this event.

Figure 9. *Artist's depiction of John Paul Jones unfurling the Grand Union flag for the first time on 3 December 1775 on the Continental Navy's flagship,* Alfred. Painting in oils by W. Nowland Van Powell, U.S. Navy Art Collection, Washington, D.C., Donation of the Memphis Council, U.S. Navy League, 1776.

In his *Memoir of the American Revolution* prepared for the king of France, Jones writes: "America has been the Country of my fond election, from the age of thirteen, when I first saw it. I had the honor to hoist, with my hands, the flag of Freedom, the first time it was displayed on the River Delaware; and I have attended it, with veneration, ever since on the ocean." Why would Jones use the term "flag of Freedom"? Aside from obvious allusions to American liberty and freedom, the context of his letter to Dutch Colonel Baron Van der Capellen was an attempt to answer the British press who Jones had thought "censured [him] unjustly." Although having been born in England, Jones explains "I do not inherit the degenerate spirit of that fallen Nation, which I at once lament and despise. It is far beneath me to reply to their hireling invectives: they are strangers to the inward approbation, that greatly animates and rewards the Man, who draws his sword only in support of the dignity of Freedom."[24]

The day before the flag's debut, Commodore Esek Hopkins accepted the position of Commander-in-Chief of the Continental Navy. On the same day, in the day book of James Wharton, a Philadelphia ship chandler outfitting the fleet, there is record of payment to flag-maker Margaret Manny for an ensign for the *Alfred*.[25] The term "ensign" is used to signify a national flag when used at sea and is customarily flown from the "position of honor" at the stern of a vessel. The design and colors of this flag can be accurately established by several primary source eyewitness accounts and other corroborating records of the period.

---

[24] John Paul Jones, *Memoir of the American Revolution Presented to King Louis XVI of France by John Paul Jones*, trans. Gerard W. Gawalt [Honolulu: University Press of the Pacific, 2001], 93.

[25] On 2 December 1775 Esek Hopkins accepted his commission as Commander-in-Chief of the Continental Navy ("Samuel Ward and Stephen Hopkins to Nicholas Cooke," reprinted in *NDAR*, Volume 2, 1233), and the day book of ship chandler James Wharton lists the quantity and cost of the fabric purchased for the *Alfred*'s new ensign with a payment to flag-maker Margaret Manny ("Cr Margt Manny for makg an Ensign £ 1.2.8"), reprinted in *NDAR*, Volume 3, ed. William Bell Clark (Washington, D.C.: Government Printing Office, 1968), 1380. John Paul Jones hoisted the Grand Union ensign for the first time on the *Alfred* the following day.

"The Continental Flag"

After twice touring "eight of the thirteen United Colonies" since the battle of Lexington, Bernard Page, a Loyalist clergyman, wrote the Earl of Dartmouth on 20 December 1775, warning of the growing colonial resolve toward independence and their capacity to secure it. The obeisant letter advances the often repeated notion of American frontiersmen being highly capable marksmen and soldiers; evidently, Page's agenda was to prevent the expansion of hostilities into a broader war by painting a dire picture for England:

> In marching through woods, one thousand of these riflemen would cut to pieces ten thousand of your best troops. I don't, my Lord, speak at random, or write partially. I have travelled too much among these men to be insensible of their abilities. O, my Lord! if your Lordship knew but one half what I know of America, your Lordship would not persist, but be instantly for peace, or resign. But, my Lord, construe this epistle as you please; nevertheless, my meaning is that it should not in the least convey, or even hint any thing about the legality or illegality of the unhappy dispute.[26]

Page also mentioned the appointment of Commodore Hopkins and the Grand Union flag's first appearance on the *Alfred*: "A Continental and Provincial currencies, to facilitate this great undertaking [war with England], are emitted, which circulate freely, and are daily exchanged for silver and gold. Their harbours by the spring will swarm with privateers. An Admiral is appointed, a court established, and the 3d instant, *the Continental flag on board the Black Prince, opposite Philadelphia, was hoisted*"[27] (emphasis added).

During the Revolutionary War, the term "continental" was used to refer to devices and institutions concerning the whole of the North American colonies; namely, the Continental Congress, continental currency, etc. By referring to it as "the Continental flag," Page seems to recognize that this flag was emblematic of the United Colonies. As we shall see, other eyewitness accounts and even pictorial evidence confirm this general understanding of what the new standard represented.

In another letter dated 6 December 1775, containing intelligence from Philadelphia, the Continental Navy's first flagship and her new flag are also mentioned: "we are fitting out here [Philadelphia] a number of ships with the greatest expedition to attack him [Lord Dunmore]; they will sail, or at least fall down the river in a few days, viz. The Black Prince [Alfred], a fine vessel, I believe you know her well, *she carries a flag* and mounts from twenty to thirty twelve and sixteen pounders, besides swivels, and fights them mostly under deck"[28] (emphasis added).

---

[26] Reprinted in Force, *American Archives*, Series 4, Volume 4, 358.

[27] Dartmouth Papers, William Salt Library, Stafford, Staffordshire, England. "Permission to reproduce the letter in full was given by the then Earl of Dartmouth to Admiral William R. Furlong." Rear-Admiral William Rea Furlong and Commodore Byron McCandless, *So Proudly We Hail: The History of the United States Flag* (Washington, D.C.: Smithsonian Institution Press, 1981), 95. Bernard Page's letter to Dartmouth can be found in Force, *American Archives*, Series 4, Volume 4, 358, and is also reproduced in *NDAR*.

[28] "The Town and County Magazine or Universal Repository of Knowledge, Instruction, and Entertainment for January, 1776," *Domestic Intelligence* (Philadelphia, 6 December 1775), 54. This letter was also published in the *Morning Chronicle and London Advertiser* on 20 January 1776.

"English Colours But More Striped"

On 4 January 1776 British spy James Brattle made a detailed spreadsheet of the newly outfitted Continental fleet comprised of five vessels led by the *Alfred* and *Columbus*—another Willing, Morris & Co. merchant ship converted to man-of-war (FIGURE 10). In his role as spy, Brattle posed as a servant to congressional delegate James Duane of New York, and evidently had access to very detailed intelligence. In his report he lists the ship's commanders, the number of marines assigned to each vessel, and their armaments. Brattle also describes a novel flag flying aboard the *Alfred*: "[Esek] Hopkins Commands the *Alfred*, she has Yellow sides, her Head the figure of a Man, *English Colours but more striped*"[29] (emphasis added).

Figure 10. *Painting in oils by W. Nowland Van Powell, depicting the* Columbus, *under the command of Captain Abraham Whipple, bringing in the British brig* Lord Lifford, *while operating off the New England coast in 1776.* USA Dept. of the Navy, Naval Historical Center, Navy League, 1776.

In context, "English colors but more striped" undoubtedly describes the Grand Union flag comprised of the British Union and thirteen red-and-white stripes. It also nicely illustrates the initial difficulty and confusion in describing the new design as either being British or American. As other historians have concluded in the absence of contradictory evidence, we can safely assume this flag to have been the "ensign" made by Margaret Manny, mentioned by Bernard Page, and hoisted by John Paul Jones on the *Alfred* on 3 December 1775.[30]

[29] "Intelligence from Philadelphia, Transmitted by Captain Hyde Parker, Jr., R.N., January 4, 1776," reprinted in *NDAR*, Volume 3, 615–616.

[30] Edward W. Richardson, *Standards and Colors of the American Revolution* (Philadelphia: University of Pennsylvania Press, 1982), 63–64: "The above entry identifies Philadelphia seamstress, Margaret Manny, as the maker of the first United Colonies ensign for the Continental Navy."

"What They Call The Ammerican Flag"

On 5 January 1776, as the nascent Continental Navy was finally ready to set sail, the Naval Committee of Congress issued orders to Commodore Hopkins. Addressed "America To Esek Hopkins Esquire, Commander in Chief of the Fleet of the United Colonies"—the orders were unequivocal in their war-making powers:

> Sir: The United Colonies directed by principles of just and necessary preservation against the oppressive and cruel system of the British Administration whose violent and hostile proceedings by sea and land against these unoffending colonies, have rendered it an indispensable duty to God, their country and posterity to prevent by all means in their power the ravage, desolation and ruin that is intended to be fixed on North America. As a part and a most important part of defence, the Continental Congress have judged it necessary to fit out several armed vessels which they have put under your command having the strongest reliance on your virtuous attachment to the great cause of America, and that by your valour, skill and diligence, seconded by the officers and men under your command our unnatural enemies may meet with all possible distress on the sea...you will send forward a small swift sailing vessel to gain intelligence of the enemies situation and strength. If by such intelligence you find that they are not greatly superior to your own you are immediately to...search out and attack, take or destroy all the naval force of our enemies that you may find there.[31]

On 10 January 1776 Gilbert Barkly, another British spy writing from Philadelphia, provided details about the American flotilla to Sir Grey Cooper "per express to New York" and mentions the Grand Union as "what they call the Ammerican Flag":

> Sir The two ships and tuo [sic] briganteens I mentioned in my last fell down the river the 4th Currt. the ships has 250 men including marine's each of them, and the Briganteens 100 men each, they are Joined by a sloop of 12 guns from New England, there is also a Briganteen, and a Sloop fitted out at Baltimore in Marry land which Joins them before they leave this river: the reason (no doubt) for their shipping such a great number of men, is that they intend to board their antagonists sword in hand: they have hoisted *what they call the Ammerican Flag viz the British Union, with thirteen stripes red and white, for its field, Representing the thirteen United Collonies* [32] (emphasis added).

Barkly's account leaves no doubt as to the design of the Grand Union flag; indeed he cites a similar term to what John Paul Jones used years later (compare "Ammerican Flag" with "Flag of America"). It is notable that Barkley mentions the colonists referring to this new flag by name, "what they call the Ammerican Flag." Both Page's and Barkly's descriptions introducing the new flag identify it as representative of a united colonial effort in opposing the British. Despite the absence of congressional records or other primary source documents revealing the Grand Union's origin or purpose, it does seem, at least anecdotally, that there were contemporary perceptions of the Grand Union flag embodying nationalistic characteristics.[33]

---

[31] "Naval Committee to Commodore Esek Hopkins, Philadelphia, 5 January 1776," *NDAR*, Volume 3, 637–638.

[32] "Gilbert Barkley to Sir Gray Cooper, 'per express to New York,' Philadelphia, January 10, 1776," *NDAR*, Volume 3, 721–722; *Pennsylvania Magazine of History and Biography* LXXXV (n.d.), 28–30, from the collection (Sir Henry Barkly Papers) of Mrs. Mona MacMillan of Long Whittenham, Berkshire, England. Sir Grey Cooper was a Member of Parliament and Secretary of the Treasury. Gilbert Barkly, once a relatively successful merchant in Philadelphia, was the consignee for the East India Company's shipment of tea to Philadelphia on Captain Ayres's tea ship, *Polly* in 1773. This ship was sent back to England avoiding the more inflammatory result that had occurred in Boston.

[33] British spy Gilbert Barkly, in an intelligence dispatch made on 20 May 1776, mentioned the Continental Navy as being referred to as the "American fleet" supporting the notion that both the fleet and its new flag embodied nationalistic characteristics. "Since my last 16th. March, the Ammerican fleet (as they are Called) arrived at New London in New England" (Seed, "A British Spy in Philadelphia," 32).

Pictorial Evidence

Images of the Grand Union flag on contemporary powder horns and illustrations of the period confirm the written descriptions.

A 10 February 1776 letter to the North Carolina Council of Safety from that state's delegates in Congress, mentions shipment "by the wagon" of, "Drums, Colours, Fifes, Pamphlets and a quantity of powder." The colors mentioned were purchased by Joseph Hewes from ship chandler James Wharton and charged on 8 February 1776. The bill is itemized as "*1 Union Flag 13 Stripes Broad Buntg and 33 feet fly*"[34] (emphasis added).

This flag was most likely flown in Edenton, North Carolina, and two months later, on 2 April 1776, the Grand Union flag was enshrined on a seven-and-a-half dollar bill (Figure 11).

The formation of a national identity—made more distinct in the face of escalating British violence—was quickly materializing. Rituals and

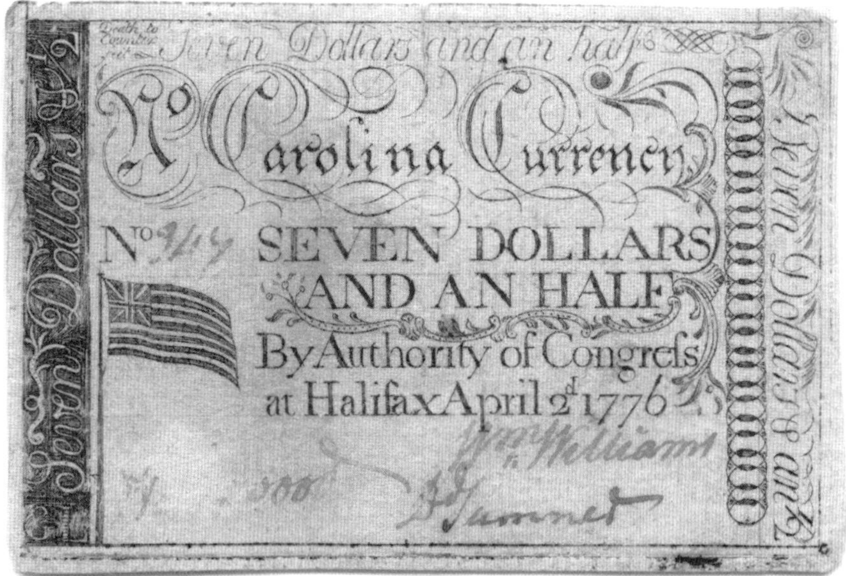

Figure 11. *Grand Union flag representative of the United Colonies displayed on North Carolina currency, dated 2 April 1776. Since its debut over the Continental Navy on 3 December 1775 and Army on 1 January 1776, the new flag was quickly adopted throughout the revolutionary enterprise.* Courtesy of Tyron Palace, New Bern, NC, accession TP.1986.032.001

symbols, some heraldic, some novel, began to encapsulate the birth of the American nation.

Four days later, on 6 April 1776, the words "united states of America" first appeared publically in print published by the *Virginia Gazette* in Williamsburg.[35]

In the summer of 1776, a watercolor painting of one of the Continental Navy's ships, Captain Wynkoop's *Royal Savage*, shows the Grand Union flag in full color (Figure 12). Although the British Union in the canton is slightly smaller than the North Carolina seven-and-a-half dollar depiction, this establishes without question what the "Ammerican flag" or "Flag of America" looked like. Because each flag was hand-sewn, most likely there were slight variations; for instance, the size of the canton usually differs in these flags.

It is conspicuous to note that many of the surviving early reports of the new device come from the British side or from unofficial accounts in the colonial press—and only a few from American decision-makers. Most of these reports are brief and perfunctory. As stated earlier, any detailed record of the Grand Union flag's adoption or purpose has yet

Figure 12. *Watercolor painting of Captain Wynkoop's* Royal Savage *displaying the Grand Union flag on Lake Champlain by Marine Lt. John Calderwood.* Manuscript and Archives Division, The New York Public Library, Astor, Lenox, and Tilden Foundations.

to be discovered. This seems to suggest one of three things—the story of the flag's origin wasn't documented; researchers have been unlucky in discovering the relevant sources; or, for various reasons, there may have been concerted documentary suppression during or after the fact.

---

[34] "Like the aforementioned "Flag of America" ensign which was hoisted by John Paul Jones on the *Alfred*, most likely this "Union Flag 13 Stripes" purchased by Joseph Hewes was also made by Margaret Manny. Hewes, a congressional delegate from North Carolina, was also on the "committee charged with fitting out its newly acquired ships. The friendship between Jones and Hewes went back to Scotland where, as John Paul, the former joined a Masonic fraternity at Kircudbright; his application was attested by James Smith. This James Smith was the brother of Robert Smith, a partner of the mercantile firm of Hewes and Smith of Edenton, North Carolina, whom James later met when he came to the colonies. Another fellow townsman from Scotland was David Sproat, who settled in Philadelphia. When Jones went from Virginia to Philadelphia in the fall of 1775 to seek employment in the ships being fitted out by the Continental Congress, letters were addressed to him in care of David Sproat. By late September or early October Jones was in Philadelphia. Joseph Hewes arrived there on October 22. On October 30, Hewes was one of the four members added to the naval committee to hasten the work of outfitting the ships of the Continental Navy. As a member of that committee, Hewes may well have called upon Jones to help with the job" (Furlong and McCandless, *So Proudly We Hail*, 90). This may explain why Jones took part in the Grand Union flag-raising on 3 December 1775 while not having officially received his naval commission until 7 December.

[35] Byron DeLear, "Who coined the name 'United States of America'? Mystery gets new twist," *Christian Science Monitor* (16 August 2012). The A PLANTER essay, number two of three, published in the *Virginia Gazette* on 6 April 1776, stands as the first publically printed evidence of the phrase "united states of America." Interestingly, Peter Force's *American Archives* describes the essay as a "political pamphlet" and in his transcription capitalizes "United States of America" whereas the *Virginia Gazette* renders it as "united states of America." The author made this discovery as part of research for this book and was published by the *Christian Science Monitor*, NBC News, Yahoo News, the UK's *Daily Mail* among others. (Reprinted in *Force, American Archives*, Series 4, Volume 5, 798; "To the Inhabitants of Virginia," *Virginia Gazette* 1287, 6 April 1776.)

"Ship. Amaraca."—First Portrayal of the Grand Union?

The earliest discovered pictorial evidence of the Grand Union flag seems to be a coarse rendering engraved on a powder horn dated 9 March 1776 (Figure 13). Major Samuel Selden's powder horn loosely depicts the British and American lines in the closing chapter of the Siege of Boston eight days before the British withdrawal.

The scrimshaw design includes an image of a three-masted warship labeled "SHIP. AMARACA." The vessel appears to be flying the Pine Tree flag on its main-mast and a union flag with thirteen stripes at its stern. This prominent portrayal of "SHIP. AMARACA." was perhaps intended as a metaphor for national unity and an abstract representation of the United Colonies—akin to Plato's proverbial "ship of state."[36] Other symbolic images on the Selden powder horn include a hefty mortar cannon most likely depicting the large brass mortar captured from the British ordnance brig *Nancy* by Captain John Manley on 28 November 1775.

Figure 13. *Earliest pictorial evidence of the Grand Union flag on Major Samuel Selden's powder horn, dated 9 March 1776.* Photo by John Bell, courtesy of the Massachusetts Historical Society.

Figure 14. Detail of the Selden powder horn showing a union flag with thirteen stripes. Although a poor rendering, it shows the intersecting crosses of St. George and St. Andrew and fourteen solid lines moving from one end of the flag or canton to the trailing edge which constitute the thirteen stripes. Photo by John Bell, courtesy of the Massachusetts Historical Society.

Flying from the position of honor, at the farthest aft staff on the vessel's stern, is a union flag with thirteen stripes, albeit poorly rendered. It is significant to note that national ensigns are customarily flown from this position—the stern of a vessel—as was the Grand Union flag since its first appearance on the *Alfred* (FIGURES 3, 5, 6 AND 9).

Several flag histories identify this flag as being the Grand Union flag; although others have indicated doubt thinking that it might reveal a different and heretofore unknown flag. The rendering thus bears detailed examination.

First, the artist was working with accuracy limitations typically associated with scrimshaw; namely, a difficult medium to work with, an abstract ad hoc composition, and a lack of readily available precise information. Additionally, the spelling of America as "AMARACA" brings the artist's level of literacy into some question only because it was such a common word seen in print; although literacy is not a bar to rendering graphic symbols such as flags. As clearly visible in Figure 14, the British Union "canton" is centered on the staff as opposed to being in the upper hoist corner of the flag, and in the middle of the flag's field, is a "cross-hatch" etching pattern, an etching technique used to indicate color and shading. As there are no Revolutionary War flags yet discovered that feature a British Union "canton" centered on its field and staff, this hints at the possibility the artist produced poor flag renderings in general. Certainly, the Pine Tree flag on the main topmast is a little coarse. Taking this into consideration, it seems that the best candidates for what the artist intended with this "striped/cross-hatch union flag" would be either a Red or Blue Ensign—or the Grand Union flag. Regarding stripes—upon closer inspection, one can see complete and uninterrupted stripes on both edges of the flag, three on top and two on the bottom. When you count all the uninterrupted "stripe lines" on the flag, including the "cross-hatched" ones, there are a total of fourteen solid lines which frame thirteen stripes. "Thirteen stripes" is one of the Grand Union's chief characteristics being "emblematical of the thirteen united colonies," and in numerous period primary sources is utilized to describe the flag. Thirteen stripes is a crucial clue which would seem to support the Grand Union flag theory—it would be more of a stretch to think that after engraving a union flag with thirteen stripes that the artist intended something other than the Grand Union flag. This pictorial evidence presents the Grand Union flag as a "national ensign" which is an important clue as to its perceived function.[37]

Presenting the Grand Union in this fashion comports with earlier eyewitness accounts describing the new colors as "what they call the Ammerican flag" or otherwise embodying nationalistic characteristics being "emblematical of the thirteen united colonies." Terms such as "Flagg of the United Colonies" and "New Provincial Flagg" in use at the time most likely referred to the new standard further supporting its perceived national character.[38] Outside the remote possibility that the Selden powder-horn artist intended to represent some other flag, this scrimshaw illustration can safely be assumed to place the Grand Union flag in Boston as a "national ensign" approximately two months after Washington's flag-raising ceremony on Prospect Hill.

---

[36] The term "ship of state" was popularized by book VI of Plato's *Republic*. Written around 380 BCE, the use of the phrase compares the governance of a city-state to the command of a naval vessel.

[37] *So Proudly We Hail* (1981) and *Our Flag Number* (National Geographic Society, 1917) consider this to be a Grand Union flag; John Bell, author and webmaster of the well-known Boston 1775, has doubts.

[38] Two other primary sources in the first quarter of 1776 support the idea of the Grand Union flag embodying nationalistic characteristics: "Minutes of the Pennsylvania Committee of Safety, dated Feb 24, 1776: "That Capt. Proctor procure a Flagg Staff for the Fort, with a Flagg of the United Colonies." (Reprinted in *NDAR*, Volume 4, ed. William Bell Clark (Washington, D.C.: Government Printing Office, 1969), 71); and, the "Diary of Major Barnard Elliot" of the 2nd South Carolina Regiment, dated 9 March 1776: "If Men of War [are sighted] the New Provincial Flagg will be hoisted & lowered as many times as there are Men of War seen." (Reprinted in *NDAR*, Volume 4, 277.) As mentioned in Peter Ansoff's "Flags of the State Navies in the Revolutionary War" (*Raven* 17 [2010]: 23–46), Captain Barnard Elliot described signal flags to report ships approaching the harbor and his 9 March 1776 entry states: "Johnsons Fort will hoist the old common blue Fort Flagg or Jack." There is cause to believe this to be the blue Crescent flag of South Carolina being that it was made in September 1775 and that the "New Provincial Flagg" mentioned in the above quote possibly referred to the Grand Union flag. The February reference "Flagg of the United Colonies" (and possibly the aforementioned "New Provincial Flagg") further establishes the contemporary perception of the Grand Union being the de facto "flag of America." Because the Grand Union was described by numerous observers in "continental" and nationalistic terms immediately before and after the flag-raising event at Prospect Hill, there's no compelling reason to think that General Washington and his staff were not aware of the new "union flag" by New Year's Day, 1776.

Prospect Hill: "We Had Hoisted the Union Flag in Compliment to the United Colonies"

Tradition has it that on New Year's Day, 1776, General George Washington unfurled what is considered the first "unofficial" flag of the United States of America to commemorate the Continental Army's "new establishment" (FIGURE 15). As has been established, this flag featured thirteen characteristic red-and-white horizontal stripes with the British Union Jack in the canton.

Figure 15. *"Raising the First American Flag" illustration by Clyde Osmer De Land under the supervision of Howard Pyle. Published by Harper's Weekly in 1898, De Land stated in an accompanying essay: "It was doubtless the union jack in the corner of the flag hoisted at Cambridge that caused the English to misinterpret it—to suppose that the Americans intended to submit once more to the rule of George the Third."* Picture Collection, The New York Public Library, Astor, Lenox, and Tilden Foundations.

The Grand Union was hoisted atop a 76-foot liberty pole on Prospect Hill—a strategically important fortified high-ground overlooking British-occupied Boston.[39] There are three primary source eyewitness accounts of the Prospect Hill flag-raising. The most famous, as Ansoff reports, was written by Washington to his military secretary, Lieutenant-Colonel Joseph Reed, three days after the event:

> Cambridge, 4th Jany 1776
>
> Dear Sir
>
> . . .
>
> We are at length favour'd with a sight of his Majesty's most gracious speech, breathing sentiments of tenderness and compassion for his deluded American subjects; the echo is not yet come to hand, but we know what it must be, and as Lord North said, and we ought to have believed (and acted accordingly,) we now know the ultimatum of British justice. The speech I send you; a volume of them was sent out by the Boston gentry, and farcical enough, we gave great joy to them (the red coats I mean), without knowing or intending it, for on that day, the day which gave being to the new army, (but before the proclamation came to hand) *we had hoisted the Union Flag in compliment to the United Colonies*; but behold! it was received in Boston as a token of the deep impression the Speech had made upon us, and as a signal of submission, so we learn by a person out of Boston last night By this time, I presume, they begin to think it strange that we have not made a formal surrender of our Lines[40] (emphasis added).

Ansoff concluded that the term "Union Flag," in this specific instance, can only allude to the British Union Jack and not the continental union flag. He states: "Washington referred simply to the 'Union Flag', and there is no indication that he meant anything other than what he said."[41]

[39] During the Siege of Boston on 1 August 1775, a tall liberty pole was erected on Prospect Hill, a fortified high-ground overlooking the road to British-occupied Boston. The 76-foot-tall liberty pole was originally a ship's mast that had been recently captured from the British armed schooner HMS *Diana*, in the aftermath of the Battle of Chelsea Creek on 27–28 May 1775.

[40] George Washington to Joseph Reed, Cambridge, 4 January 1776, in *The Writings of George Washington from the Original Manuscript Sources 1745–1799*, ed. John C. Fitzpatrick, Vol. 4 (Washington, D.C.: Government Printing Officer, 1931), 210–211.

[41] Peter Ansoff, "The Flag on Prospect Hill," *Raven* 11 (2006): 77–100.

The Grand Union is a "Union Flag"

In modern parlance, it would be correct to assume the term "union flag" most likely refers to the British Union Jack—especially from a flag-expert or flag-centric perspective. The British Union Jack is featured prominently in vexillology as it can be found, even today, incorporated into the design of many of the world's flags. But in the American Revolutionary War, the meaning and usage of the word "union" is not so easily ascertained. The argument could be made that the more pertinent "union" in the minds of American Founders, and, perhaps, even the British, was the one taking shape.

Nevertheless, notions of how the word "union" was employed by both British and American actors during the revolutionary era are issues of nuance and will be explored later, because there is a far more compelling argument that brings Ansoff's theory into question. Simply, the striped continental union flag was exactly that—a Union Flag.

The problem with interpreting Washington's account from a strictly modern and/or literalist point of view, is that there are numerous references to the Grand Union flag during the months preceding and following Prospect Hill that utilize the exact same language—albeit some more descriptive and complete than others. This establishes, through primary source records, the linguistic convention of referring to the Grand Union as a "union flag." Contemporary observers used the term "union flag" to identify the new striped colors—not the "old colours" which were often referred to as "English colours" or the "English flag." In fact, the majority of contemporary primary sources during the period of its introduction refer to the new striped continental as a "union flag."

Here is a list of primary source references to the Grand Union flag using the term "union":

- "Union Flag" (12 December 1775)[42]
- "UNION FLAG of the American States" (15 May 1776)[43]
- "Union flag, and striped red and white in the field" (2 December 1775)[44]
- "Continental Union Flag" (11 May 1776)[45]
- "1 Union Flag 13 Stripes Broad Buntg and 33 feet fly" (8 February 1776)[46]
- "union flag with thirteen stripes in the field emblematical of the thirteen United Colonies" (9 February 1776)[47]

- "a Continental Union Flag" (20 April 1776 and 20 June 1776)[48]
- "striped under the union with thirteen strokes" (3 March 1776 and multiple citations)[49]

These descriptions (FIGURE 16) are strikingly similar to Washington's own eyewitness account, "we had hoisted the Union Flag in compliment to the United Colonies." In fact, it bears repeating that *any flag* including the British Union in its design could have been called a "Union Flag."

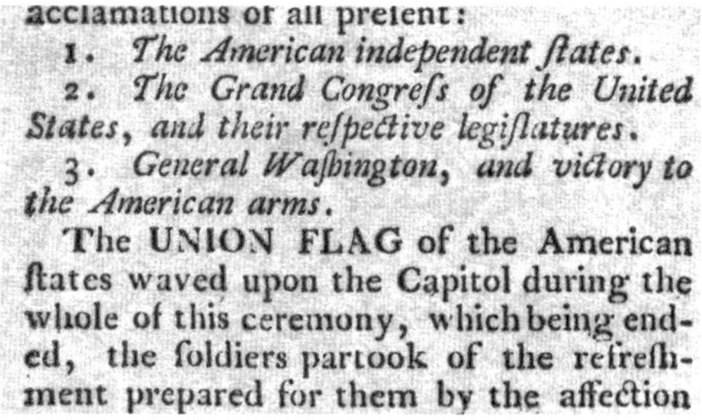

acclamations of all preſent:
1. *The American independent ſtates.*
2. *The Grand Congreſs of the United States, and their reſpective legiſlatures.*
3. *General Waſhington, and victory to the American arms.*

The UNION FLAG of the American ſtates waved upon the Capitol during the whole of this ceremony, which being ended, the ſoldiers partook of the refreſhment prepared for them by the affection

Figure 16. *Photographic excerpt from the Virginia Gazette dated 17 May 1776 using the term "UNION FLAG" to describe the Grand Union flag. It was "waved upon the Capitol" of Williamsburg during a celebration following a public reading of the 15 May unanimous vote by the Virginia Convention declaring the United Colonies "Free and Independent States."* The Colonial Williamsburg Foundation.

One key example among these descriptions is the 12 December 1775 reference to "Union Flag" because it uses the exact abbreviated description that Washington used in his account of the flag raising on Prospect Hill. Ansoff concluded Washington's account to indicate a British Union flag rather than the new striped continental, or Grand Union flag. The 12 December record is from Philadelphia ship chandler James Wharton's account book. Wharton's account book lists items procured for the outfitting of the first Continental Naval fleet consisting of two ships, two brigs, and a sloop (*Alfred*, *Columbus*, *Cabot*, *Andrew Doria*, and *Providence*). As mentioned, John Paul Jones had the distinction of hoisting what he termed the "Flag of America" (the Grand Union flag) for the first time on the *Alfred* on 3 December 1775. The 12 December reference lists "1 Union Flag" procured for the second ship of the Continental Navy, *Columbus*, which displaced 200 long tons and mounted 28 guns.

Dr. John Hattendorf, a professor of maritime history at the U.S. Naval War College and an expert on sailing warships of the revolutionary era, reviewed this reference. He concluded that "1 Union Flag" for the Columbus on 12 December 1775, could only refer to the Grand Union flag, as any "old colours," namely, the British Red Ensign or British Union flag, were readily available and not needed for the initial outfitting of the Continental Navy's first flotilla.[50]

Another key example of the contemporary usage of the term "Union Flag" to describe the striped Grand Union can be seen in a photographic excerpt from the Virginia Gazette newspaper dated 17 May 1776 (FIGURE 16). The pertinent phrase stands out due to being rendered in all capitalized letters: "The UNION FLAG of the American States waved upon the Capitol during the whole of the ceremony [...]" This demonstrates unequivocally that Americans used the term "union flag" to describe the new national symbol.

As primary source records show, British Red, Blue, or White Ensigns could also be referred to as "union flags." Dated 8 March 1775, the following is an "Account of the Meetings" that took place in New York concerning the decision to send delegates to the Continental Congress:

> Early on *Monday* morning preparations were made for the meeting at the Exchange. *A Union Flag, with red field*, [emphasis added] was hoisted on the Liberty-pole, where, at nine o' clock, the friends of Freedom assembled, and having got in proper readiness, about eleven o' clock the body began their march to the Exchange. They were attended by musick; and two standard bearers *carried a large Union Flag, with a blue field*, [emphasis added] on which were the following; inscriptions: On one side, *George* III.—*Rex* and the Liberties of *America*—No Popery. On the other: The Union of the Colonies, and the Measures of Congress.[51]

Figure 17. *The British Red Ensign was used by the Royal Navy and British merchant vessels. One theory about the Grand Union posits its relatively easy creation by applying six white stripes to an existing Red Ensign.* Daderot (username), commons.wikipedia.org.

While the Red Ensign (a.k.a "Meteor Flag" or "Red Duster"), Blue Ensign, and Grand Union flags all have British Unions in their cantons, the difference between these flags is their fields. The Red Ensign's field is all red (FIGURE 17) and the Blue Ensign's field all blue, while the Grand Union's is striped. In any event, as the above account shows, these flags could all be referred to as "union flags." At the time of the introduction of the new striped union flag this was the best abbreviated way to describe it.

Therefore we must conclude that it was entirely suitable for Washington and others to have referred to the Grand Union flag as a

"Union Flag." Ironically, as Ansoff writes, "there is no indication that he [Washington] meant anything other than what he said," is actually true. But Washington wasn't describing an "English flag" or the "King's standard"—he was summoning the most available descriptive term at the time—the striped continental colors was a "union flag."

It is noteworthy that contemporary accounts using the term "union" could have either been motivated by the most prominent feature of the flag, the British Union Jack, or by the thirteen stripes intimating the union of the colonies—or both. To wit, the reason Washington used the term "union" might have been different than why the other two eyewitnesses—both British—used the term "union."

---

[42] The 12 December record is from Philadelphia ship chandler James Wharton's account book and can be found in *NDAR*, Volume 3, 1382.

[43] The *Virginia Gazette* 68 (17 May 1776) (A. Purdie, printer) used the term "UNION FLAG" to describe the Grand Union flag: "The UNION FLAG of the American states waved upon the capitol during the whole of this ceremony, which, being ended, the soldiers partook of the refreshment prepared for them by the affection of their countrymen, and the evening concluded with illuminations, and other demonstrations of joy; every one seeming pleased that the domination of Great Britain is now at an end, so wickedly and tyrannically has it been exercised for these twelve or thirteen years past, notwithstanding our repeated prayers and remonstrances for redress."

[44] "Letters of Delegates to Congress: Volume 2, September 1775–December 1775, Naval Committee to the Virginia Convention, written by Richard Henry Lee," reprinted in *NDAR*, Volume 3, 640–641, and dated 5 January 1776. However, as Ansoff mentions, there is evidence to suggest this letter was written in December 1775, perhaps as early as 2 December, the day before the Grand Union's unveiling. If so, it stands as the first detailed description of the Grand Union flag. The Library of Congress website transcribes the date of this letter as 2 December, while the University of Virginia transcription leaves out the day, but indicates the month: "Philadelphia [December ?, 1775]." This confusion was primarily due to the fact that the fleet could not set sail due to ice and freezing conditions despite being ready in December. A footnote to "Letters to Delegates to Congress" states that Lee left it [the date] blank, "apparently in the expectation that it would be filled in later, and in which passages referring to vessels ordered to the Chesapeake are cast in the past tense, suggesting that the letter was to be sent when the fleet was ready to sail and the orders for its commander were ready." The fleet eventually cast off on 5 January. In the letter, Lee informs the Virginia Convention of the creation of the Continental Navy's first flotilla, a "small fleet of Armed Vessels," intended to "seize and destroy as many of the Enemies [sic] ships and Vessels as they can." To facilitate this mission, Lee makes the request for "a Person of unquestioned honor, understanding, and secrecy" to board the fleet when it arrives off the Capes of Virginia and provide the commander-in-chief with enemy intelligence. For the purposes of identification, Lee lists the fleet as consisting of "Two Ships, two Brigateens, and one Sloop,"—but for greater certainty in identifying the Americans—"the largest Ship [*Alfred*] will carry at her Mizen Peak a Jack with the Union flag, and striped red and white in the field."

[45] "Resolution of the Conventon [sic] of Virginia, Williamsburgh, May 11, 1776," reprinted in Force, *American Archives*, Series 4, Volume 6, 462: "On *Wednesday* last the honourable Convention of this Colony came to the unanimous resolution of giving instruction to our Delegates in Congress, at *Philadelphia*, to propose a final separation of these Colonies from *Great Britain*, by declaring them free and independent States. The day following the troops in this city, with the train of artillery, were drawn up, and went through their firings and various other military manoeuvres [*sic*], with the greatest exactness; a Continental union flag was displayed upon the Capitol, and in the evening many of the inhabitants illuminated their houses." A photographic image of the *Virginia Gazette* renders the pertinent phrase as, "continental union flag" (*Virginia Gazette* 1293 [18 May 1776], 3.)

[46] "North Carolina Delegates in the Continental Congress to the North Carolina Council of Safety," reprinted in *NDAR*, Volume 3, 1205: "The colors [Grand Union flag] referred to were purchased by Joseph Hewes, from James Wharton, ship chandler, and charged for February 8, 1776. The bill is itemized in James Wharton's Day Book, HSP, and reads: 1 Union Flag 13 Stripes Broad Buntg and 33 feet fly."

[47] "Account of the sailing of the first American fleet, Newborn [*sic*], North-Carolina, February 9, 1776," reprinted in Force, *American Archives*, Series 4, Volume 4, 964: "They sailed from Philadelphia amidst the acclamations of many thousands assembled on the joyful occasion, under the display of a Union Flag, with thirteen stripes in the field, emblematical of the Thirteen United Colonies."

[48] *Virginia Gazette* (20 April 1776), 3: "Williamsburg, April 20: The Roebuck has taken two prizes in Delaware bay, which she decoyed within her reach by hoisting a Continental Union Flag, one containing 7000 stands of arms and quantity of ammunition, the other linens, &c. To counterbalance this disagreeable piece of news, soon after she had sailed with her prizes, a cargo of 1100 casks of gunpowder got safe up to Philadelphia." This report was republished in the *Pennsylvania Evening Post* dated 20 June 1776.

[49] "Striped under the union with thirteen strokes" appears in several publications in various forms between March and late July 1776: "March 3, 1776. The colours of the American fleet (under Commodore Hopkins, which plundered the island of new Providence) were striped under the Union with 13 strokes, called the Thirteen United Colonies" (Henry B. Dawson, ed., *The Historical Magazine and Notes and Queries Concerning the Antiquities, History and Biography of America*, Vol. 3, Second Series [Morrisania, N.Y.: Henry B. Dawson, 1868], 299); "Letter from New Providence, Bahamas (after the Continental fleet's raid on New Providence)," dated 13 May 1776, printed in *London Ladies' Magazine* (July 1776): "The colors of the American fleet were striped under the Union, with thirteen strokes called the United Colonies, and their standard, a rattlesnake; motto—'Don't Tread on Me!'" (Naval History and Heritage Command, http://www.history.navy.mil); *Public Advertiser* dated Friday, 19 July 1776: "York, July 16…The Colours of the American Fleet were striped under the Union with 13 strokes, called the Thirteen United Colonies" (reprinted in William James Morgan, ed., *Naval Documents of the American Revolution*, Volume 6 [Washington, D.C.: Naval History Division, 1972], 477); and the *Edinburgh Evening Courant*, 22 July 1776: "The colours of the American fleet were striped under the Union with 13 strokes, called the Thirteen United Colonies" (*Edinburgh Evening Courant*, 22 July 1776, 2). George Henry Preble in his seminal works, "Our Flag…" (1872) and "History of the Flag…" (1880) transcribes "strokes" as "stripes."

[50] Hattendorf is the Ernest J. King Professor of Maritime History at the U.S. Naval War College and is credited with assisting the online publication of the *Naval Documents of the American Revolution* on www.navalrecords.org.

[51] "Account of the Meetings on the Evenings of Thursday, Friday and Saturday Last, and on Monday Morning, the 6th Instant, When it was Determined, by Large Majorities, to Send Deputies to a Provincial Congress Authorized to Choose Delegates to the Next Continental Congress," New York, Wednesday, 8 March 1775, reprinted in Force, *American Archives*, Series 4, Volume 2, 358.

Joseph Reed: Washington's Favorite Military Secretary

To further understand Washington's choice of words it is important to take into consideration the intended recipient of the letter. Was Washington attempting to make an exact description, like a historian or flag-expert to a neutral party? Or was the recipient sufficiently familiar with the issues at hand? And if so, how familiar?

Ansoff described Washington's account of the Prospect Hill flag-raising as a "letter to his friend," and while Lt. Col. Joseph Reed was certainly a friend of Washington's, their association was largely professional. Their well-known correspondence of the period covered highly sensitive military topics, prevailing political concerns, and operational details of the office of Commander-in-Chief of the Continental Army.

Figure 18. *Lt. Col. Joseph Reed accompanied Gen. Washington from Philadelphia to Cambridge to take command of the Continental Army. Reed worked closely with Washington in reforming what were largely New England militia into the "new establishment"—the Army of '76.* Source: Courtesy of Pennsylvania Capitol Preservation Committee, http://cpc.state.pa.us

On 15 June 1775 Congress appointed Washington commander-in-chief and dispatched him to Boston to take command of what Washington called "the Troops of the United Provinces of North America." He arrived shortly after the Battle of Bunker Hill—for the British, one of the bloodiest encounters of the entire war. At that time the continental forces besieging the British were loosely formed and composed mainly of New England militias and what the redcoats termed "country people." Lt. Col. Joseph Reed (Figure 18) accompanied Washington on his journey from Philadelphia and discovered "the Army was a scene of disorder and confusion…the Officers were not only ignorant and litigious, but scandalously disobedient, and in the last action [Bunker Hill] many of them proved such notorious cowards that the very existence of the army, and consequently the salvation of America, depended upon immediate reform."[52]

The task at hand for Washington and his aides and staff was daunting as the Americans were faced with confronting the full force of British military might, and to put it simply, they weren't ready. Washington wrote: "An Army without Order, Regularity & Discipline, is no better than a Commission'd Mob," and for the nascent force to achieve any measure of success he needed to unite and pull men together from different colonies into one coherent fighting unit.[53]

The challenge was herculean and those closest to the general feared he might collapse under its weight. Reed was Washington's right-hand man and the general trusted him implicitly. He resided with Washington at his Cambridge headquarters (now Longfellow House) and was intimately involved in every aspect of the commander-in-chief's duties. Washington often referred to Reed as a member of "his family."[54] During this critical period of reformation, Reed mentions "everyone around him [Washington] in whom he could confide" assisted him "to execute this necessary work." Reed worked side-by-side with Washington, issuing orders, writing letters, sitting in council—all from within the confines of Washington's headquarters. He was committed to see him through this "sea of difficulties."[55]

Aside from building and ensuring the integrity of their defensive lines against the British, their primary goal was to reform the ragtag provincial troops into what would be considered the first real Continental Army. Upon Washington's recommendations and other considerations, the Continental Congress in Philadelphia issued regulations, commissions, and orders for the new army just like it had done for the new navy.[56]

After spending the summer and early autumn at Washington's side in Cambridge, Reed returned to Philadelphia on 29 October 1775. Washington kept diligent contact with Reed who often times acted as the general's agent and confidant in dealings with the Continental Congress. It is impossible to divorce the orders, directives, and intelligence contained in Reed's papers from the most critical aspects of the prosecution of the revolutionary enterprise—in a phrase, like Washington, he was at the heart of the matter.

Ten days before departing Cambridge for Philadelphia, Reed wrote one of only a handful of surviving explicit flag directives of the period.

Addressing Colonel Glover and Stephen Moylan, esq. at Salem, Reed makes the suggestion of utilizing the Pine Tree flag so "our vessels may know one another." He describes the "particular Colour" as a flag "with a white ground, a Tree in the Middle, the motto (*Appeal to Heaven*)[.] This is the Flag of our floating Batteries."[57]

Thus, Washington and Reed were not only aware of and concerned with the colors the continentals would be flying, but were also involved in deciding which flags would be used. When Washington wrote Reed on 4 January relaying the story of the Prospect Hill flag-raising ceremony, it can safely be assumed Reed knew to what Washington was referring when he said "we had hoisted the Union Flag in compliment to the United Colonies." Their close working relationship on these matters likely may have obviated the need for additional clarifying detail.

Flag historian Edward W. Richardson, in his *Standards and Colors of the American Revolution*, reached a similar conclusion. He mentioned Reed was at Washington's side while they met with the Congressional Committee sent to confer on the needs and budget of the Army in October 1775. Richardson concludes "Washington did not describe the flag to Reed. He speaks of it only as 'the union flag' which indicates that Reed knew the design."[58]

Ansoff disagreed, adhering to a new interpretation of what Washington meant when writing Reed: "All modern accounts assume that the flag to which Washington referred was the Continental Flag of 13 stripes with the British union in the canton. Neither his words or the context would seem to support this assumption."[59]

First, it is not only "all modern accounts" of the event at Prospect Hill that depict the Grand Union flying there, but all the secondary sources of the period, newspaper articles, etc. report the same conventional history, and, if erroneous, nowhere were they later corrected until Ansoff. Additionally, Washington's words *do* "support this assumption," and consequently, support the conventional history—that the Grand Union flag was flown that day to commemorate the army's new establishment. Again, contemporary primary sources show that Washington's words—"union flag"—were many times employed to describe the new American colors.

[52] Martin I. J. Griffin, *Stephen Moylan: Muster-Master General Secretary and Aide-de-Camp to Washington Quartermaster-General Colonel of Fourth Pennsylvania Light Dragoons and Brigadier-General of the War for American Independence* (Philadelphia: Garrett Press, 1909), 9.

[53] George Washington, General Orders, Head Quarters, Cambridge, 1 January 1776, in *The Writings of George Washington from the Original Manuscript Sources, 1745–1799*, ed. John C. Fitzpatrick, Volume 4, 202.

[54] Letter from General Washington to Joseph Reed, urging his return to Head-Quarters: "Cambridge, January 23, 1776. DEAR SIR: Real necessity compels me to ask you, whether I may entertain any hopes of your returning to my family." (Reprinted in *Force, American Archives*, Series 4, Volume 4, 831.)

[55] Griffin, *Stephen Moylan*, 9.

[56] On 29 September 1775 "the Continental Congress resolved: That a Committee of three members of this Congress be appointed to repair immediately to the camp at Cambridge, to confer with General Washington, and with the governor of Connecticut, and the lieut-Governor of Rhode Island, the council of Massachusetts, and the President of the convention of New Hampshire, and such other persons as to the said Committee shall seem proper, touching the most effectual method of continuing, supporting, and regulating a continental army. The next day, the Congress chose 'Mr. Lynch, Dr. Franklin, and Mr. Harrison' to comprise that committee" (J. L. Bell, *General George Washington's Headquarters and Home—Cambridge, Massachusetts* [Damascus, Md.: Penny Hill Press Inc., U.S. Department of Interior, 2012], 540). Washington, his generals, representatives from several colonies, and this congressional oversight committee sat in council for five days in Washington's army headquarters on 18–22 October 1775. The civil-military conference generated plans, pay and regulations for the new army.

[57] "Colonel Joseph Reed to Colonel John Glover and Stephen Moylan, Salem, Head Quarters (Cambridge), 20 October 1775," reprinted in *NDAR*, Volume 2, 538.

[58] Edward W. Richardson, *Standards and Colors of the American Revolution* (Philadelphia: University of Pennsylvania Press, 1982), 267: "Lt. Col. Joseph Reed, Washington's Secretary in 1775, had returned to his native Philadelphia in late 1775. He had been with the Congressional Committee which conferred with Washington on needs and budget for the Army in October 1775. It was to Reed that Washington wrote his often quoted January 4, 1776 letter which mentioned the hoisting of the 'Union' flag before Boston on January 1, 1775 [*sic*, 1776]. Washington did not describe the flag to Reed. He speaks of it only as 'the union flag' which indicates that Reed knew the design."

[59] Ansoff, "The Flag on Prospect Hill," 84

"Which Is Here Supposed to Intimate the Union of the Provinces"

The second eyewitness account of the New Year's Day flag-raising at Prospect Hill was an anonymous British merchant ship captain writing his ship's owners in London. Dated 17 January 1776, he wrote: "I can see the Rebels' camp very plain, whose colours, a little while ago, were entirely red; but, on the receipt of the King's speech, (which they burnt,) they have hoisted the Union Flag, *which is here supposed to intimate the union of the Provinces"*[60] (emphasis added).

As mentioned earlier, this use of the term "Union Flag" by a British subject might have been motivated by different reasons than why Washington used the term. What the British reacted to was the transition from an "entirely red" device to a union flag of any type, striped or otherwise. Indeed, in Washington's letter to Reed, the general mentions the confusion caused to the British by the flag-raising ceremony on Prospect Hill.

Washington relays that the British mistakenly thought the King's speech made the Americans have a change of heart. As a consequence, the rebel's colors transition from an "entirely red" flag—a common signal for protest, duress, and rebellion—toward that of a British Union (albeit striped in the field).[61] From a British perspective, it must have been the weight of royal authority wielded by their Sovereign that precipitated the shift from rebellious red flag to the loyal "union flag."[62]

As indicated by Washington, this was confused, and, perhaps, wishful thinking on the part of the British. It was an emotionally satisfying interpretation—sighting the British Union atop the rebels' camp gave the red coats the false hope that they might not be forced to carry out a bloody campaign with the provincials after all. Most likely memories of the carnage at Bunker Hill still featured prominently in their thinking.

William Carter, a British officer of the 40th Regiment of Foot, commented in his diary on the unrelenting industry of the Continental Army and the desperate living conditions the British were suffering under (the following entry was made the day before the flag-raising at Prospect Hill):

> Boston, 31st December, 1775.
>
> On the 11th instant, the remainder of the troops on Boston Common went into winter quarters, as did also the troops on Charles-Town Heights. The cold is so intense, that the ink freezes in the pen whilst I write by the fire-side; yet, notwithstanding the severity of the season the Provincials are still at work. They are throwing up a redoubt on the hill, from whence our Light Infantry and Grenadiers took some cattle last month...This day puts a period to the year; and happy should I be to have it in my power to say, it also did to this most unhappy contest. Our little army has suffered severely from the dampness and season, and from living totally on salt provisions, without the smallest portion of vegetables.[63]

Lt. Carter's somewhat despondent attitude reveals a frame of mind that would welcome any hopeful sign. That sign came a day later in the form of a "union flag (above the continental with the thirteen stripes)," and for a brief period, the hoisting of this flag over the rebel's camp was construed by the British as indicative of a war avoided.

This complete misreading of the Prospect Hill event by the British is not so unusual and is actually supported by recent neurological research into the visual cortex. The brain's perception of reality shows a very real propensity for people to basically see what they want to see, akin to someone hallucinating an oasis in the middle of the desert while dying of thirst. These studies show that what we perceive is heavily influenced by what we are searching for with test subjects quite literally morphing their perception of time and space to reach emotionally satisfying conclusions.[64] This may offer an explanation as to why the new flag was so confusing—for the reluctant and emotionally fatigued British, the Grand Union was the sign of capitulation they were desperately hoping for. This "potent mechanism of sensory noise filtration" provided a blinkered view of the impact the king's speech had had on the Americans—because the British were so focused on the Union flag that the Americans raised, it's quite possible they simply didn't see the stripes.[65]

But the actual effect the King's speech had on the Americans was quite the opposite. In reality, George III's threats of violence only hardened American resolve toward independence.[66] There is even documentary evidence that seems to suggest this transition taking place in the minds of those present.

[60] "Extract of a Letter from a Captain of an English Transport at Boston to his Owners," reprinted in *Force, American Archives*, Series 4, Volume 4, 710.

[61] Ansoff mentions this "entirely red" flag as possibly being Israel Putnam's regimental flag (3rd CT) as do other flag histories. If so, this flag had the "armorial bearings of Connecticut," with an abbreviation for "Qui Trastulit Susinet" on one side and the words "An Appeal To Heaven" on the reverse. Nevertheless, from a distance, it still could have been perceived as "entirely red," and functioned as such for both armies. It is possible it was just a "plain" red flag as described by the anonymous ship captain whose report was reprised by later secondary sources. Red flags were used in Rome as a military signal for the *Comitia Centuriata* to assemble on the Field of Mars, and, upon an enemy's approach, the flag would be struck as a signal to prepare for battle. It was used as a signal for assembly in the American colonies, as a letter written by Governor Bernard from 1768 mentions, "The Sons of Liberty request all those, who in this Time of Oppression and Distraction, with well to, and would promote the Peace, good Order, and Security of the Town and Province, to assemble at Liberty Hall, under Liberty-Tree, on Tuesday the 14th Instant, at Ten o' Clock Forenoon, precisely…—And in that Consequence thereof, a Red Flag was hoisted Yesterday in the Afternoon at Liberty-Tree" (*Letters to the Ministry from Governor Bernard, General Gage, and Commodore Hood. And also Memorials to the Lords of the Treasury from the Commissioners of the Customs. With Sundry Letters and Papers Annexed to the said Memorials* [Boston: Edes and Gill, 1769], 120). A red flag is also mentioned in a British report during the American Revolutionary war: "Pearson spied through the morning haze a red flag flying over old Scarborough Castle on the Yorkshire coastline. The red flag signaled, 'Enemy on Our Shores'" (Evan Thomas, *John Paul Jones: Sailor, Hero, Father of the American Navy* [New York: Simon & Schuster, 2003], 179.) The Marquis De Lafayette, a very dear friend of Washington and a recent hero of the American Revolution, raised a red flag on the Champ de Mars (Field of Mars) in 1791 in Paris to indicate a state of martial law. Because the red flag was an established signal for "enemy on our shores" and used as a general signal for emergency, duress, or rebellion, Putnam's nearly all-red regimental flag would have added import and be entirely appropriate for use on Prospect Hill during the Siege of Boston while the continentals reformed while besieging the "enemy on our shores."

[62] The anonymous merchant ship captain's report mentions the "Rebels" burning the King's speech. Being that the account was dated more than two weeks after the Prospect Hill flag-raising, it shows the British were eventually disenthralled of their initial reaction to the hoisting of the Grand Union flag and that the King's speech was not received warmly by the Americans.

[63] Lt. William Carter, *A genuine detail of the several engagements, positions, and movements of the Royal and American armies: with an accurate account of the blockade of Boston and a plan of the works on Bunker's Hill, at the time it was abandoned by His Majesty's forces* (London, n.p., 1785; reprinted by Sabin America Print Editions 1500–1926).

[64] Emily Balcetis and David Dunning, "See What You Want to See: Motivational Influences on Visual Perception," *Journal of Personality and Social Psychology* 91 (2006): 612–625: "People's motivational states—their wishes and preferences—influence their processing of visual stimuli. In 5 studies, participants shown an ambiguous figure (e.g., one that could be seen either as the letter B or the number 13) tended to report seeing the interpretation that assigned them to outcomes they favored. This finding was affirmed by unobtrusive and implicit measures of perception (e.g., eye tracking, lexical decision tasks) and by experimental procedures demonstrating that participants were aware only of the single (usually favored) interpretation they saw at the time they viewed the stimulus. These studies suggest that the impact of motivation on information processing extends down into preconscious processing of stimuli in the visual environment and thus guides what the visual system presents to

conscious awareness." Wharton Marketing, "Motivated Visual Perception: Seeing What We Want to See," marketing.wharton.upenn.edu: "People assume that their visual experiences accurately reflect reality. Research in our lab questions this supposition. Instead, we argue that motivational forces color the perceptual representations that reach perceivers' awareness. Data suggest that higher-order social motivations originally considered relevant to the domain of social thought—motives such as wishful thinking, cognitive dissonance, and desires—bias visual perception."

[65] Sarah Harrison, "Do We Only See What We Want To See? Experts Don't Notice A Gorilla In Their Midst," 21 July 2013, Science 2.0 (http://www.science20.com).

[66] Thomas Paine in a revised edition of his popular pamphlet "Common Sense" commented on the king's speech delivered to the Continental Army on New Year's Day, 1776: "Since the publication of the first edition of this pamphlet, or rather, on the same day on which it came out [10 January 1776 in Philadelphia], the king's speech made its appearance in this city. Had the spirit of prophecy directed the birth of this production, it could not have brought it forth at a more seasonable juncture, or at a more necessary time. The bloody-mindedness of the one, shows the necessity of pursuing the doctrine of the other. Men read by way of revenge: and the speech, instead of terrifying, prepared a way for the manly principles of independence" (Thomas Paine, *Common Sense; Addressed to the Inhabitants of America* [Philadelphia: W. and T. Bradford, 1776], 37). Paine further describes the speech in an article printed on 27 March 1776 in the *New England Chronicle*: "The Speech if it may be called one, is nothing better than a wilful [*sic*] audacious libel against the truth, the common good, and the existence of mankind; and is a formal and pompous method of offering up human sacrifices to the pride of tyrants. But this general massacre of mankind is one of the privileges, and the certain consequence of Kings; for as nature knows them NOT, they know NOT HER, and although they are beings of our OWN creating, they know not US, and are become the gods of their creators. The Speech hath one good quality, which is, that it is not calculated to deceive, neither can we, even if we would, be deceived by it. Brutality and tyranny appear on the face of it." In his article, Paine possibly alludes to Washington's own opinion of independence: "I shall chiefly confine my farther remarks to the following heads. First. That it is the interest of America to be separated from Britain. Secondly. Which is the easiest and most practicable plan, RECONCILIATION OR INDEPENDANCE? With some occasional remarks. In support of the first, I could, if I judged it proper, produce the opinion of some of the ablest and most experienced men on this continent; and whose sentiments, on that head, are not yet publicly known." Washington in a letter to Reed in January mentions independence and Paine's popular and persuasive pamphlet: "A few more of such flaming arguments, as were exhibited at Falmouth and Norfolk, added to the sound doctrine and unanswerable reasoning contained in the pamphlet "Common Sense," will not leave numbers at a loss to decide upon the propriety of a separation" (George Washington to Joseph Reed, Cambridge, 31 January 1776, in *The Writings of George Washington from the Original Manuscript Sources 1745–1799*, Vol. 4, 297).

"Full and Ample Powers from the United States of America"

On 2 January 1776, the day after Prospect Hill and the receipt of the King's speech, Washington's aide-de-camp and Muster-Master General of the Continental Army, Stephen Moylan, esq., wrote what stands as the first documentary evidence of the phrase "United States of America."[67] Written to Lt. Col. Joseph Reed, Moylan's letter (FIGURE 19) makes clear that notions of independence were on the minds of the men operating in the heart of the revolutionary enterprise. He laments the fact that Congress has yet to declare independence, despite—for all intents and purposes—their "Most Gracious Majesty" accusing them of as much: "Look at the King's speech—it is enclosed in this, or in the General's letter to you…—will they [Congress] not declare what his Most Gracious Majesty insists on they have already done?"[68]

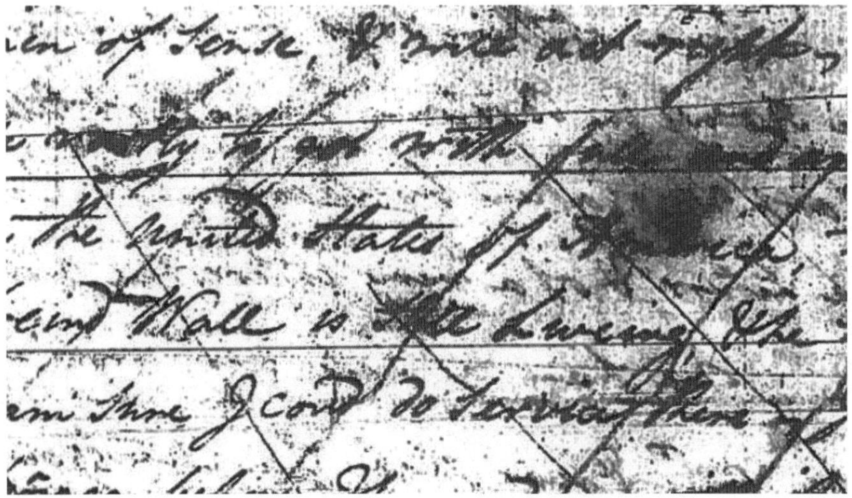

Figure 19. *Detail of Stephen Moylan, esq., letter to Lt. Col. Joseph Reed showing the first documentary evidence of the phrase "United States of America." Moylan, Washington's aide-de-camp, wrote Reed from Washington's Cambridge headquarters on 2 January 1776—the day after the Prospect Hill flag-raising.* Collection of the New York Historical Society.

Moylan then expresses his fervent desire to carry the "full and ample powers from the United States of America" to Europe to assist in the war effort. Whether precipitated by the King's speech, the flag-raising

Figure 20. *Painting in oil on canvas by studio of Allan Ramsay, 1763 of King George III of Great Britain in coronation robes*. National Galleries of Scotland.

at Prospect Hill, or by other reasons, Moylan's shift from using the term "United Colonies" toward "United States of America" strongly suggests the congealing of an American national identity at that very moment.[69]

Historian Joseph Ellis, in his *Revolutionary Summer: The Birth of American Independence*, mentions John Adams's belief that his primary collaborator in swaying Congress toward independence was King George himself (Figure 20). The king's bellicose speech was delivered to the continentals on New Year's Day, and in the months following, played a pivotal role in what amounted to the English king's tone-deaf handling of the American crisis:

> MANY YEARS LATER, when John Adams was asked who deserved the lion's share of the credit for advancing the agenda toward independence in the Continental Congress, most of the questioners assumed that Adams would make a gesture of modesty, then claim the honor for himself. But he relished surprising them by bestowing the prize on George III. He was undoubtedly referring to the royal proclamation issued in August 1775 and the king's address to both houses of Parliament the following October…By the start of the new year, then, George III had single-handedly undermined the reconciliation agenda of the moderate faction in the congress. For the moderates had invested all their hopes in a wise and loving monarch whose paternal affection for his American subjects would eventually bring the warmongers in the ministry and Parliament to their senses. Now George III had demonstrated that he was perhaps the most

ardent advocate for war in the British government. The king had seized the initiative himself, and his advisers promptly lined up behind their sovereign. While the moderates were busy blocking any declaration of American independence from the British Empire, George III had in effect issued his own declaration of independence from them.[70]

---

[67] Byron DeLear, "Who coined 'United States of America'? Mystery might have intriguing answer," *Christian Science Monitor*, 4 July 2013. On 2 January 1776 a letter to Lt. Col. Joseph Reed—Washington's favorite military secretary—was composed in the Continental Army Headquarters at Cambridge. The author was Stephen Moylan, esq., the Muster-Master General of the Continental Army, and in Reed's absence, Washington's aide-de-camp. While assisting the general the two men had lived with him in the Army Headquarters in Cambridge as members of—as Washington put it—"his family." Moylan wrote that he wished to carry the "full and ample powers from the United States of America" to Europe to assist in the revolutionary enterprise—most likely procuring much needed armaments and gunpowder. Their shortage of powder so desperate, at one point, orders had actually been issued to use wooden harpoons instead of guns. Moylan, born in Cork, Ireland, had been educated in Paris and worked in the shipping business in Lisbon before becoming a merchant in Philadelphia. He had partnered with many prominent business leaders in Philadelphia including co-owning a ship with Robert Morris, "the financier of the American Revolution." Moylan's experience as a merchant is what prompted another leading Philadelphian, John Dickinson, to write a letter of reference paving the way for the Irish immigrant's appointment as Muster-Master General of the Continental Army (George Washington to John Dickinson, Camp at Cambridge, 30 August 1775, in *The Writings of George Washington from the Original Manuscript Sources 1745–1799*, Vol. 3, 459).

[68] Moylan letter as detailed in n67.

[69] On Christmas Day, 1775—eight days before his "USA" letter—Washington's aide-de-camp Stephen Moylan, esq., inscribed on the flap of a document, "On the service of the United Colonies." The day after Prospect Hill, on 2 January 1776, Moylan expressed his wish "to take the full and ample powers from the United States of America" to Spain to assist in the revolutionary enterprise (see 67).

[70] Joseph J. Ellis, *Revolutionary Summer: The Birth of American Independence* (New York: Alfred A. Knopf, 2013), 10–11.

"The Continental with the Thirteen Stripes"

The third eyewitness account of the Prospect Hill flag-raising, also British, was made by the aforementioned Lieutenant William Carter, 40th Regiment of Foot. Dated a few weeks after the event, he documented the Continental Army celebrating the appearance of a "union flag (above the continental with the thirteen stripes)" at Prospect Hill on New Year's Day:

> Boston, 26th January, 1776.
>
> The Provincials have entered on the new year with spirit.
>
> The King's speech was sent by a flag [of truce] to them on the 1st instant. In a short time after they received it, they hoisted *an union flag (above the continental with the thirteen stripes*) at Mount Pisga [Prospect Hill] their citadel fired thirteen guns, and gave the like number of cheers[71] (emphasis added).

Because Lt. Carter's eyewitness account mentions the "continental with the thirteen stripes," it may be the most illuminating primary source with regard to answering the question of whether the Grand Union flag really flew at Prospect Hill.

Ansoff concludes that Carter is describing *two* distinct flags. He states: "Unlike the other two eyewitnesses, Lt. Carter mentions 'thirteen stripes.' However, it seems fairly clear from his phrasing that he is talking about a Union Flag flying above another, striped flag. As with the anonymous ship captain, Carter's correspondents in Britain would not have any reason to think that 'union flag' meant anything different from what it usually meant."

We have already established in contemporary primary sources that the Grand Union flag was referred to as a "union flag" for various reasons, including it being emblematic of the union of the colonies, and, like the Red Ensign, could be described as a "union flag" due to the fact it had a British Union in its design. Setting aside for the moment the fact that stripes flew at Prospect Hill, Ansoff's conclusion from this account that *two* flags were present that day would make this report entirely unique among all relevant primary and non-derivative secondary sources.[72] However, there is another, and perhaps more plausible interpretation of Lt. Carter's narrative which conforms to the conventional history.

Contemporary sources describe the positioning of a flag's "field" as contrasted with the positioning of the "canton" in various ways. One way to describe the field and/or canton was to portray it as being in a superior and/or inferior position to one another. Just as much as the field of a flag could be described as "below" or "under" the canton, the canton could be described as "above" the field (Figure 21).

One source showing this positioning convention was from 3 March 1776 and reprinted in numerous publications until late July 1776: "The colours of the American fleet (under Commodore Hopkins, which plundered the island of new Providence) *were striped under the Union with 13 strokes, called the Thirteen United Colonies*"[73] (emphasis added). And another, possibly drawn from the same source: "Letter from New Providence, Bahamas (after the Continental fleet's raid on New Providence), dated 13 May 1776, printed in *London Ladies' Magazine*, July 1776: 'The colors of the American fleet were *striped under the Union*, with thirteen strokes called the United Colonies, and their standard, a rattlesnake; motto—Don't Tread on Me!'"[74] (emphasis added).

Taking this philology into account, Lt. Carter's report of "an union flag (above the continental with the thirteen stripes)" could be interpreted as describing one flag—the Grand Union flag, which, from a positioning perspective, has the British Union Jack above and in a superior position to the field of stripes below (Figure 21).

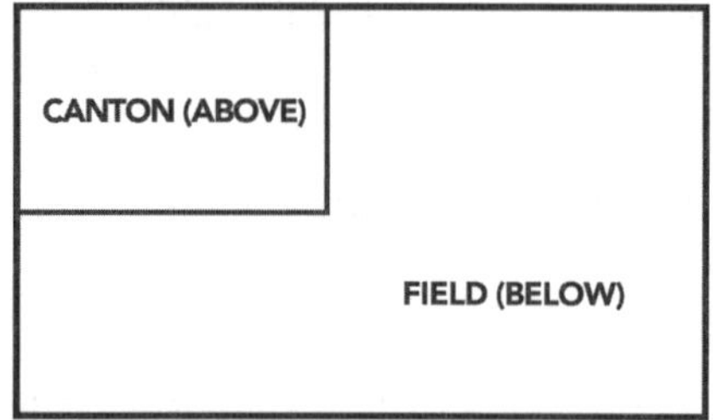

Figure 21. *Diagram showing the positioning of a flag's canton in relation to its field.* Illustration created by the author.

Contemporary language describing the positioning of the canton and field was not confined to the above/below convention as the following record illustrates. Here, the Grand Union's canton is described as being "next" to the staff: "(COPY) July [29] 1776...Sir I arrived here the 27th Instant between one and two o'clock, and immediately waited upon the Governor of this place, and deliver'd your Message, which he sent to the General of the Island at Port Royal, and the same evening returning from him a little before Dark I saw a Sail in the Offing with Colours which I was unacquainted with (*being red and white striped, with a Union next the Staff*) "[75] (emphasis added).

[71] Lt. William Carter wrote: "A genuine detail of the several engagements, positions, and movements of the Royal and American armies: with an accurate account of the blockade of..." (Lt. William Carter, *A genuine detail of the several engagements*). The semi-colon after Mount Pisga has been removed according to publisher's notes at the end of Carter's diary publication.

[72] Following the two-flag conclusion, Ansoff suggests the second flag could have been a "striped signal flag." He writes that, "One can only speculate about what, if any, flag was really hoisted under the Union Flag on that historic day. Perhaps it was one of the signal flags that were commonly flown on Prospect Hill. Washington might have simply failed to mention it because it was not pertinent to the point he was making to Reed. Carter, on the other hand, might have seen a striped signal flag and assumed, in light of the salutes and cheers, that it was intended to represent the colonies."

[73] Dawson, *The Historical Magazine*, Vol. 3, Second Series, 299. (See n49 for a complete listing of publications citing this account.)

[74] Naval History and Heritage Command (http://www.history.navy.mil).

[75] "Captain John Chapman, R.N., to Vice Admiral James Young, Shark in Fort St. Pieres Bay, Martinico, [29] July 1776," reprinted in *NDAR*, Volume 5, 1278.

George Washington: Careful, Calculating, Cautious

Many historians have written about the political and public character of George Washington, that he was careful, cautious, and calculating, and that he was uniquely aware of his place at the center of the American Revolutionary stage and played his part excellently (FIGURE 22).

Two additional ideas brought forward by Ansoff deserve reflection. One is that in the years running up to the revolutionary era, English colonists sometimes flew British Union Jacks with words like "Liberty" emblazoned on them as a "symbol of united resistance to British policies," and the other is, that at the time of Prospect Hill, the commander-in-chief (or anyone else in Boston) had not yet heard about the Grand Union flag's existence.

Figure 22. *George Washington by Rembrandt Peale, ca.1850. Washington conspicuously wore the uniform of a Virginian colonel at the Continental Congress in Philadelphia, and was appointed Commander-in-Chief of the Continental Army in 1775.* National Portrait Gallery, Washington, D.C., via DcoetzeeBot (username), commons.wikipedia.org.

Early examples of British American colonists flying British flags are provided by Ansoff, ostensibly to set the stage and give credence to his Prospect Hill theory that a wholly British device was flown on New Year's Day, 1776. The example with the latest date he provides is from a British officer's diary on 1 May 1775 following the outbreak of hostilities at Lexington and Concord: "The Rebels have erected the Standard at Cambridge; they call themselves the King's Troops and us the Parliaments. Pretty Burlesque!"

This confirms that Americans sympathetic to the colonial cause flew English colors—there is no question about this. However, these examples are of actions that were conducted in a relatively *ad hoc* manner as contrasted with the Grand Union flag's debut on the *Alfred*, or Washington's Prospect Hill ceremony inaugurating the army's "new establishment." They occurred before the bloody escalation at Bunker Hill and the appointment and command of Washington as commander-in-chief—two developments that necessitated heightened levels of military discipline, seriousness, and formality.

As mentioned earlier, the massive challenge associated with organizing the new army of '76 took place from July 1775 until the downbeat of the new establishment on New Year's Day (and efforts at reform continued thereafter). During this time, the war was escalating throughout the colonies, with ships and stores seized, forts captured, and cities burned. It was a harrowing autumn and winter; and Washington was facing the very real deadline of army commissions closing out at the end of the year.

Historian Paul K. Longmore, in *The Invention of George Washington*, likens the general's role during this time as an orchestrator of implicit "acts of sovereignty":

> In October, a congressional committee huddled with him [Washington] at Cambridge to hear his recommendations. The alterations he proposed would move the United Colonies much farther down the road toward independence. Congress adopted every one. The army would be augmented. Courts-martial would have authority to enforce stricter discipline by imposing stricter punishments. Captured British spies would face the death penalty. Mutiny and sedition by officers and soldiers in the Continental Army would now also be tried as capital crimes. These last two acts, voted by Congress in the first week of November, were implicitly acts of sovereignty by an independent nation. They had originated with the commander-in-chief.[76]

On New Year's Day, the day of the flag-raising ceremony on Prospect Hill, Washington issued orders from Cambridge communicating his opinion of the nature and character of the new army: "This day giving commencement to the new army, *which, in every point of View is entirely Continental*, the General flatters himself, that a laudable spirit of emulation will now take place, and pervade the whole of it. Without such a spirit, few officers have ever arrived to any degree of reputation, nor did any army ever become formidable" (emphasis added).

The formality and official nature of the occasion is unambiguous. Washington, as a well-known Freemason (along with many of his generals), was accustomed to strict adherence to ritual and ceremony as not only being a question of virtue, but one of honor (FIGURE 23). For Washington, the dawning of what would become known as the "Revolutionary Year" was significant—he was inaugurating the new army he had pained so tirelessly to build. The surrounding circumstances seem to suggest the perfect opportunity for the flag's disclosure—it seems unimaginable that he would fly the enemy's colors on this historic occasion.

In a 2009 *Boston Globe* article by Danielle Dreilinger, Suffolk University historian Robert Allison also disagrees with Ansoff's revisionist Prospect

Figure 23. *Artist's depiction of George Washington leading an elaborate Masonic ceremony laying the cornerstone for the U.S. Capitol on 18 September 1793. Washington was a well-known Freemason and recognized the importance of ceremony, ritual, and symbolism.* Allyn Cox, oil on canvas, 1973–74, Architect of the Capitol.

Hill flag theory: "Enlistments for the all-volunteer army expired Dec. 31, 1775; Washington was issuing a call to arms for the forces to keep them all from going home. 'Raising the flag is a sign' of differentiation and change in this context, Allison said. 'Washington, probably more than any of his contemporaries, knew the importance of symbols.' During the siege of Boston, the rebels made a mental transition from angry Brits to independent Americans."[77]

Washington's orders on New Year's Day capture the intensity and integrity of what he wanted to impart to his men of the "new establishment":

> His Excellency hopes that the Importance of the great Cause we are engaged in, will be deeply impressed upon every Man's mind, and wishes it to be considered, that an Army without Order, Regularity and Discipline, is no better than a Commission'd Mob; Let us therefore, when every thing dear and valuable to Freemen is at stake; when our unnatural Parent is threat'ning of us with destruction from every quarter, endeavour by all the Skill and Discipline in our power, Discipline in the continental army to acquire that knowledge, and conduct, which is necessary in War—Our Men are brave and good; Men who with pleasure it is observed, are addicted to fewer Vices than are commonly found in Armies; but it is Subordination and Discipline (the Life and Soul of an Army) which next under providence, is to make us formidable to our enemies, honorable in ourselves, and respected in the world; and herein is to be shewn the Goodness of the Officer.[78]

In light of the seriousness of the occasion, Washington's attention to issues of formality, and the aforementioned deliberate "acts of sovereignty" that had originated with him, it would be wholly uncharacteristic for him to hoist the King's colors, a British Union Jack—a flag completely English in design—in a celebration to commemorate the Continental Army's new establishment. Doing so would seem haphazard, nay, even capricious, and is plainly not supported by the surrounding circumstances. As Massachusetts Institute of Technology historian Pauline Maier succinctly summarized in the *Globe* piece, "You wouldn't want a flag that was the same flag as the people [you were fighting]."[79]

This is why Washington was *surprised* by the British reaction to Prospect Hill and found it hilarious—to wit, if he had hoisted a wholly English flag, *of course* it would be seen as a token of submission and/or loyalty to the British. It wouldn't be ironic—it would be obvious. But the humorous tone of his 4 January letter to Reed was based on the confusing message the new flag unwittingly transmitted (being composed of both British and American elements).[80] Washington was delighted to report the unintended effect that the new flag had on the "redcoats"—a flag, by the way, which Reed was most certainly well aware of, which brings us to the second issue.

Ansoff suggests that Washington was "probably not aware" of the existence of the first flag of America when Washington wrote Lt. Col. Joseph Reed about Prospect Hill and the King's speech: "The Continental Flag was created in Philadelphia for use by the embryonic Continental Navy. It was never officially adopted or promulgated, and there is no mention of it in any of Washington's extensive correspondence with the Continental Congress between July and December of 1775. When he wrote his letter to Reed, Washington was probably not even aware that it existed."[81]

First, we do not have direct evidence about the Grand Union's provenance; therefore, its creation story should not be narrowly confined solely to the purpose of "use by the embryonic Continental Navy." If this were true, the Grand Union flag would not have been used as a garrison flag in February 1776 at Fort Mifflin (Fort Island), or as the standard hoisted by the American troops during July in New York (FIGURE 24).[82]

Additionally, it would be inaccurate to claim that the Grand Union flag "was never officially adopted or promulgated" only that we don't have *direct evidence* of its adoption. On the other hand, its promulgation throughout the colonies is self-evident.

Lastly, because there is an absence of primary source documents detailing Washington's awareness of the new standard does not mean he didn't know of its existence. Indeed, there is no mention of the flag in Washington's "extensive correspondence" with Congress between July and December 1775, but this only adds to the vacuum of *any* evidence about the Grand Union's provenance beyond the brief accounts in a smattering of primary sources.

Washington was the Commander-in-Chief of the Continental Army and was at the heart of the revolutionary enterprise. If a British spy, writing on 10 January 1776, mentions the Grand Union as "what they call the Ammerican flag," it is not too far of a stretch to presume—at the very least—that knowledge of that flag (and what it evidently represented) had passed from Philadelphia to Cambridge among principals of

Plate 1. *Artist's depiction of John Paul Jones unfurling the Grand Union flag for the first time on 3 December 1775 on the Continental Navy's flagship*, Alfred. Painting in oils by W. Nowland Van Powell, U.S. Navy Art Collection, Washington, D.C., Donation of the Memphis Council, U.S. Navy League, 1776.

Plate 2. *"Raising the First American Flag" illustration by Clyde Osmer De Land under the supervision of Howard Pyle. Published by Harper's Weekly in 1898, De Land stated in an accompanying essay: "It was doubtless the union jack in the corner of the flag hoisted at Cambridge that caused the English to misinterpret it—to suppose that the Americans intended to submit once more to the rule of George the Third."* Picture Collection, The New York Public Library, Astor, Lenox, and Tilden Foundations.

Downman (1685)

Lens (1700)

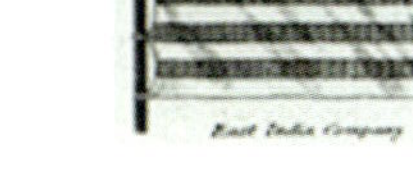

Rees (1820)

Lauri (1842)

National Geographic (1917)

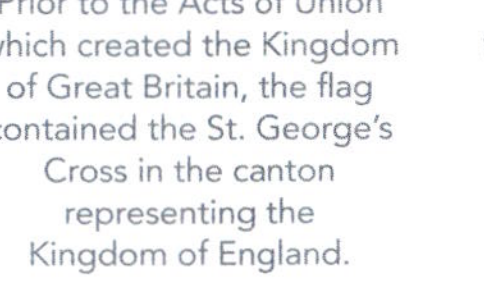

Prior to the Acts of Union which created the Kingdom of Great Britain, the flag contained the St. George's Cross in the canton representing the Kingdom of England.

The flag had a Union Flag in the canton after the creation of the Kingdom of Great Britain in 1707.

After 1801, the flag contains the Union Flag of the United Kingdom of Great Britain and Ireland in the canton (1810).

Plate 3a. *Compilation of various East India Company (EIC) flags with an evolving British canton and the number of stripes varying from 9 to 13. The EIC's pivotal role in the beginnings of the American Revolution (Boston Tea Party), in addition to the similarity between the company's colors and the Grand Union flag has intrigued historians for years. Although no causal relationship has been found, there is evidence that Benjamin Franklin and Robert Morris—two key decision makers related to the debut of the Grand Union flag—were business associates with officers of the East India Company.* Wikipedia.

Plate 3b. *Illustration of the Grand Union flag featuring the British Union Jack and thirteen red and white stripes symbolizing the union of the American colonies. Considered the "first flag of America," the Grand Union was first displayed on the Continental Navy's flagship,* Alfred, *on 3 December 1775 and was in use until late 1777.* Courtesy of Duane Streufert for USFlagDepot.com

Plate 4. *Revolutionary War re-enactors stand at attention during the Prospect Hill flag-raising ceremony in Somerville, Massachusetts, on 1 January 2011. The annual event commemorates General George Washington's unfurling of the "first flag of America," known as the Grand Union flag, at the dawning of America's Revolutionary Year.* Dave Rutherford, courtesy of House of Motion.

Plate 5. *Watercolor painting of Captain Wynkoop's* Royal Savage *displaying the Grand Union flag on Lake Champlain by Marine Lt. John Calderwood.* Manuscript and Archives Division, The New York Public Library, Astor, Lenox, and Tilden Foundations.

Plate 6. *In October and November 1776, Denmark and the Republic of the United Netherlands were, respectively, the first foreign nations to salute the new American colors—the Grand Union flag. This painting depicts the Continental Navy brig* Andrew Doria *receiving a gun salute from the Dutch fort at Sint Eustatius on 16 November 1776.* Donation of Colonel Phillips Melville, Navy Art Collection, Naval History and Heritage Command.

Plate 7. *"Drawn by Benjamin Franklin" — French color woodblock print, possibly created by Benjamin Franklin while in France in 1776-1777. It depicts the "Grand Union" as the first American flag.* Private Collection / Archives Charmet / Bridgeman Images

Plate 8. *The* Adler Von Lubeck *was the most powerful warship of its time (circa 1565) and featured red-and-white stripes on its hull and banners. It was the flagship of the* "Queen of the Hanseatic League" *(a.k.a. the city of Lubeck). The* Hanseatic League *was a vast trading network of Northern European cities that operated under Lubeck Law (circa 1226)—governance by a council of merchants as opposed to regional monarchs, dukes or kings.* Marinemaler Olaf Rahardt: www.marinemaler-olaf-rahardt.de

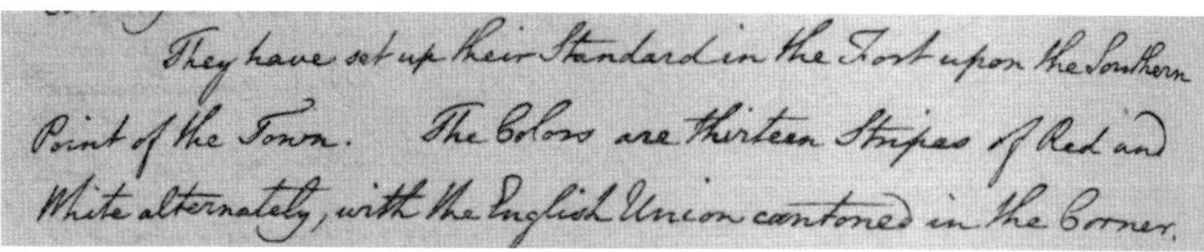
They have set up their Standard in the Fort upon the Southern Point of the Town. The Colors are thirteen Stripes of Red and White alternately, with the English Union cantoned in the Corner.

Figure 24. *Detail of facsimile of letter from Ambrose Searle to the Earl of Darmouth on 25 July 1776, stating "They have set up their standard in the fort upon the southern end of the town. Their colours are thirteen stripes of red and white, alternately, with the English Union cantoned in the corner."* Library of Congress Manuscript Division.

the American war effort. After all, they *were* the ones being accused of calling the new device "the Ammerican flag."

Further, Bernard Page's 20 December description of the *Alfred*'s ensign as "the continental flag" also establishes the general awareness of the new standard's function and purpose, as do the February minutes from the Pennsylvania Committee of Safety calling the Grand Union the "Flagg of the United Colonies."

In the weeks and months following these initial reports, the Grand Union flag began appearing throughout the colonies. As discussed earlier, it was most likely etched on Samuel Selden's powder horn on 9 March 1776—and in the first week of April was engraved and presented as a symbol of national unity on colonial currency. For the times, relatively speaking, a rapid rate of adoption.

In an anonymous report of the British retreat from Boston, eight days after the Selden powder horn's etching, there is mention of an "Ensign Richards carrying the standard" upon the Continental Army's entry into the newly evacuated city.[83] Because we've established through several earlier contemporary records the perception of the Grand Union flag as a national emblem, there is every reason to conclude (as have previous histories) that Ensign Richards was carrying the Grand Union "standard" as the Continental Army entered Boston after the British retreat.[84]

In defense of Ansoff, there is no direct evidence of Washington "knowing" about the existence of the Grand Union flag by 1 January 1776, but there may be a good explanation. The fact remains that key Washington documents and papers were purposefully suppressed and/or destroyed, and along with them, possibly, our Grand Union creation story.

[76] Paul K. Longmore, *The Invention of George Washington* (Los Angeles: University of California Press, 1988), 191.

[77] Danielle Dreilinger, "Unfurling History of Prospect Hill," *Boston Globe*, 31 December 2009 (online edition).

[78] George Washington, General Orders, Head Quarters, Cambridge, 1 January 1776, in *The Writings of George Washington from the Original Manuscript Sources, 1745–1799*, ed. John C. Fitzpatrick, Volume 4, 202.

[79] Dreilinger, "Unfurling History of Prospect Hill."

[80] There is also the possibility the Grand Union flag—as a transitional device—was intentionally created with ambiguous components communicating conflicting loyalties. If this is the case, Washington's letter to Reed was confirming the intended and/or anticipated effect.

[81] Ansoff, "The Flag on Prospect Hill," 77–100.

[82] George Canby and Lloyd Balderston, *The Evolution of the American Flag* (Philadelphia: Ferris & Leach, 1909), 35: "The letter is a long one, dated July 25th, 1776, and contains the following passage: 'They have set up their standard in the fort upon the southern end of the town. Their colours are thirteen stripes of red and white, alternately, with the English Union cantoned in the corner.'" This reference to the Grand Union flag flying over an American fort in New York is also reprised in Samuel Abbott's *The Dramatic Story of Old Glory* (New York: Boni and Liveright, 1919), 25: "Ambrose Searle, Confidential Secretary of Admiral Lord Howe of the British Navy, in a letter written July 25, 1776, spoke of the Grand Union flag at New York" and cites the same quote as Canby and Balderston. The Ambrose Searle letter is also referenced in *A Guide to Manuscripts Relating to American History in British Depositories: Reproduced for the Division of Manuscripts of the Library of Congress: "Ambrose Serle [sic] to the Earl of Dartmouth, A. L. S. New York Harbor, off Staten Island. July 25, 1776. No. 2040"* (Washington, D.C.: Library of Congress Manuscript Division, 1946), 213. The primary source is: "Ambrose Searle to the Earl of Dartmouth, July 25, 1776," facsimile in *B. F. Stevens's Facsimiles of Manuscripts in European Archives Relating to America, 1773–1783*, 24 (London: Malby & Sons, 1889), 2040.

[83] "Account of General Howe's Retreat From Boston, Cambridge, March 21, 1776," reprinted in *Force*, *American Archives*, Series 4, Volume 5, 422.

[84] The rank of ensign traditionally denotes the junior officer charged with bearing the ensign colors, or national flag. In Noah Webster's, *An American Dictionary of the English Language* (New York: S. Converse, 1828), 671, "ensign" is described as "The officer who carries the flag or colors, being the lowest commissioned officer in a company of infantry."

Washington's Missing Papers

It is an ongoing and fascinating mystery that history has yet to discover any primary source evidence of when the Grand Union flag's adoption was decided upon, or more importantly, the purpose behind the design. As mentioned earlier there are a few letters between members of Washington's staff covering the details of specific flags—Washington's secretary Lt. Col. Joseph Reed wrote one of these flag directives (to Stephen Moylan, etc.) during the period in question.

Conspicuously, there are numerous Reed letters to Washington covering this critical period that are missing from the record. We know these letters existed because Washington references them in his correspondence with Reed and they have never been found.[85] Additionally, there is evidence of concerted documentary suppression of Washington's papers which go beyond the missing Reed letters. It goes without saying, that "unknown unknowns" are exactly that—we don't know what we're missing, only that there is strong evidence of at least one individual culling Washington's papers. Colonel Tobias Lear V, Washington's secretary from 1784 to 1799, was in possession of the Washington papers for a full year after he died. Lear was also present when Washington died in December of 1799 recording his last words, "'tis well" (FIGURE 25).

Figure 25. *Colonel Tobias Lear V was Washington's secretary from 1784 to 1799. He handled many of Washington's personal affairs and was at his side throughout the Washington presidency.* Portrait by Constantina Coltellini, Courtesy of the R.W. Norton Art Gallery, Shreveport, Louisiana.

In Richard Zacks's *The Pirate Coast: Thomas Jefferson, the First Marines, and the Secret Mission of 1805* we find the story of the mishandling of Washington's papers in the year following his death:

> Now came [Tobias] Lear's least finest hour: the missing Washington papers. The case plays out like a whodunit. Instead of nephew Bushrod,

> Supreme Court Justice John Marshall wound up volunteering to write a biography of George Washington. He received the papers from Lear, who had kept them for a year. Marshall, who didn't examine the whole trunk of papers right away, was quite upset when he discovered swaths of Washington's diary were missing, especially sections during the war and presidency, and that a handful of key letters had also vanished.
>
> Lear, in a long rambling letter to Marshall, denied destroying any of Washington's papers, but Lear's own correspondence would later surface to refute his own denial.
>
> A letter has survived that Lear had written Alexander Hamilton to offer to suppress Washington documents.
>
> "There are, as you well know," Lear had written, "among the several letters and papers, many which every public and private consideration should withhold from further inspection." He specifically asked in the letter if Hamilton wanted any military papers removed. (Interestingly, while almost all the presidential diary is gone, Washington's entries for his New England trip to Lear's family home have survived.)[86]

Lear may have been carrying out a "dying wish" in removing specific documents, acting on wishes from Martha Washington, or operating on his own accord; or perhaps, all of the above. What we do know is that the twelve missing Reed letters from November to December 1775, in addition to other Washington documents and correspondence that may have been suppressed, could very plausibly have contained historical details about the Grand Union flag.

---

[85] "Dear Sir, Your letters of the 4th from New York—7th and—from Philadelphia (the last by Express) are all before me" (George Washington to Joseph Reed, Camp at Cambridge, 20 November 1775, in *The Writings of George Washington from the Original Manuscript Sources 1745–1799*, Vol. 4, 103). As cited by the National Archives these two letters from Reed are missing. From George Washington to Joseph Reed, Cambridge, 27th Novr 1775. "Dear Sir, Your Letter of the 16th by post now lyes [*sic*] before me," As cited by the National Archives this 16 November 1775 letter from Reed is missing. Similarly, the National Archives cites additional missing Reed letters from 15, 17, 20, 21, and 28 November and 2, 7, 8, and 11 December 1775. These numerous missing letters cover a critical period of time immediately preceding and following the Grand Union's first unveiling on the Delaware on the Continental Navy's flagship *Alfred*. Reed was author of one of the only flag directives of the immediate period. Further, there may be additional missing Washington letters or documents that aren't referenced explicitly, but were culled by Tobias Lear or merely lost.

[86] Richard Zacks, *The Pirate Coast: Thomas Jefferson, the First Marines, and the Secret Mission of 1805* (New York: Hyperion, 2005), 218.

Conclusions

The mystery of The First American Flag's origins has flummoxed vexillologists for nearly two centuries. The Grand Union flag's missing creation story may have been washed away attached to other documents that, for unknown reasons, were never allowed to see the light of day. Or, there may have been specific concerns about the Grand Union flag itself that coerced the record of its adoption to be suppressed. These are at least two plausible explanations for the lack of historical evidence for such an important national icon. Other possible explanations include the records merely being lost or that no notes were taken when the flag issue was decided upon. It must be remembered that the topic of independence was a highly sensitive one and even deadly in as much as openly professing and actively opposing the crown could invite charges of treason.

The Founders were doing a delicate dance and although historians have identified many different "Rubicons" and points of "no return" for the Americans toward independence, waving around a new national standard and promiscuously identifying it as such may have been perceived premature by those attempting to traipse lightly on the issue of separation with their "unnatural threatening parent." After all, the Continental Navy's creation (October 1775) and Prospect Hill's New Year's Day 1776 flag-raising ceremony both occurred before the publication of Thomas Paine's *Common Sense*, which made plain and popular the arguments against not only the English parliament, but, for the Americans, their neglectful sovereign. It is not an insignificant fact that the very public and outspoken cheerleader on these points was relatively unknown.

What this book establishes is that the Grand Union flag was referred to as a "Union Flag" in contemporary primary sources thereby bringing into question any conclusion that eyewitnesses to Prospect Hill were undoubtedly reporting a wholly British device. Further, one eyewitness mentions the "striped continental" as flying that day (with an accompanying gun salute) which also confirms the conventional history.

The advanced stage of formality and organization carried by the Americans, brought on by escalating British violence and the accelerating war preparations, likewise points toward the conventional history of the Grand Union flag hoisted in a ceremony to commemorate the new army. This conclusion is further supported by Washington's character and personal attention to issues of formality, ritual, and his stated intention to build a new force—like the Grand Union flag itself—that was representative of the United Colonies. After all, the topic of American independence and notions of nationhood were clearly maturing in this exact time and space with the first documentary evidence of the phrase "United States of America" being written at Washington's headquarters immediately following the flag-raising ceremony at Prospect Hill.

We have also seen that before the flag-raising on Prospect Hill, the Grand Union flag was seen as a national standard embodying nationalistic characteristics and throughout late 1775 and early 1776 it quickly promulgated throughout the colonies. There is evidence it was utilized as a garrison flag in February and July; it was depicted as a national ensign in Boston in March; and enshrined as a national symbol on continental currency in April. In Edenton, North Carolina, it flew courtesy of congressional delegate Joseph Hewes. In May, the Grand Union flag played a central role in celebrating colonial independence flying above the capitol of Virginia. By the end of 1776, the Grand Union flag was uniformly recognized as the de facto American colors by foreign nations (FIGURE 26).

Although British Union flags at an earlier period had been displayed by Americans in connection with united opposition to British policies, by New Year's Day 1776 things had progressed far beyond the *ad hoc* nature of the actions led by groups like the Sons of Liberty, et al. The preponderance of reports and sightings of the new American flag immediately before and after Prospect Hill make the King's colors flying there highly dubious. As an extraordinary claim, it requires more than linguistic interpretation from an era when orthography was clearly not established, not to mention any of the rigors employed by modern historians. The inexactitude of eighteenth-century language is notorious and researchers should be careful not to take a modern literalist point of view when interpreting primary source accounts. Because of the lack of direct narrative, this book has had to explore the historical context and corroborating records to divine what the few Grand Union primary sources are really saying.[87]

The Founders carefully metabolizing the issue of separation was perhaps one of the reasons the Grand Union flag's specific design was

Figure 26. *In October and November 1776, Denmark and the Republic of the United Netherlands were, respectively, the first foreign nations to salute the new American colors—the Grand Union flag. This painting depicts the Continental Navy brig* Andrew Doria *receiving a gun salute from the Dutch fort at Sint Eustatius on 16 November 1776.* Donation of Colonel Phillips Melville, Navy Art Collection, Naval History and Heritage Command.

adopted. With the British Union featured in the canton, it was plausibly deniable that designs for an "independent empire" were being harbored and actively pursued by the leaders of the rebellion. The ambiguity of the flag's design could be seen as a sort of "hedged bet." There are other possibilities, of course, including the Grand Union flag's nearly identical resemblance to the East India Company colors.

In many ways, unpacking the origin story of the Grand Union flag has allowed for the uncovering of a remarkable period of national formation. What is noteworthy is the fact that in less than one month's time we see the congealing of an American national identity as embodied by specific milestones and symbols which unequivocally communicated a sense of independence and sovereignty. From 3 December 1775 to 2 January 1776, ceremonies were conducted which heralded the inauguration of the Continental Navy, the unfurling of the first American flag, the new establishment of the Continental Army, and a new name, the "United States of America," was written for the first time.

Modern historians often have to dispel myth and legend and debunk inaccuracies to arrive at more academically-sound history. But this doesn't mean that such efforts can sometimes overreach. Doubtless, this will be a continuing discussion and, hopefully, an undiscovered repository of revolutionary war documents will soon be revealed illuminating the provenance of this most interesting national treasure, the first flag of the United States of America, the Grand Union flag.

[87] David Koeller, PhD, Professor of History at North Park University, Chicago, Ill., "Using Historical Sources, http://www.unc.edu/~branhunz/hist151/documents/Hist151ReaderFall.pdf: "Primary Sources do not speak for themselves, they have to be interpreted. That is, we can't always immediately understand what a primary source means, especially if it is from a culture significantly different from our own. It is therefore necessary to try to understand what it means and to figure out what the source can tell us about the past."

Appendix A: Grand Union and the East India Company

The Grand Union flag, composed of thirteen red-and-white stripes with the British Union in its canton, is nearly identical to the flag utilized by the British East India Company in use in one form or another for 150 years prior to the Grand Union's adoption as the "first flag of America."

Downman (1685)

Lens (1700)

Rees (1820)

Lauri (1842)

National Geographic (1917)

Prior to the Acts of Union which created the Kingdom of Great Britain, the flag contained the St. George's Cross in the canton representing the Kingdom of England.

The flag had a Union Flag in the canton after the creation of the Kingdom of Great Britain in 1707.

After 1801, the flag contains the Union Flag of the United Kingdom of Great Britain and Ireland in the canton (1810).

Figure 27. *Compilation of various East India Company (EIC) flags with an evolving British canton and the number of stripes varying from 9 to 13. The EIC's pivotal role in the beginnings of the American Revolution (Boston Tea Party), in addition to the similarity between the company's colors and the Grand Union flag has intrigued historians for years. Although no causal relationship has been found, there is evidence that Benjamin Franklin and Robert Morris—two key decision makers related to the debut of the Grand Union flag—were business associates with officers of the East India Company.*

Although we do not have any "smoking gun" evidence of any direct connection between these two flags—aside from their nearly identical appearance—examining the business interests and connections between East India Company principals and key revolutionary leaders may begin to illuminate a track connecting the two. Certainly, as the following records will show, there was at least a comprehensive awareness of the East India Company's affairs and interests held by both Robert Morris and Benjamin Franklin—two American decision makers positioned to have been instrumental in any decision to adopt the striped flag as our "national" standard (FIGURE 27).

Morris was the previous owner of the first flagship of the Continental Navy which debuted the Grand Union flag, in addition to being the procurator (through Willing, Morris & Co.) of the wharves and staging area where the first fleet was outfitted (FIGURE 9). The day before the Grand Union debut on the *Alfred*, Esek Hopkins accepted the position of commander-in-chief of the new navy and orders were given by Congress to send a military detachment to the "wharves of Messrs. Willing and Morris...to take care of the ships and stores belonging to the United Colonies." The following day, the hoisting of the Grand Union ensign on the *Alfred* essentially inaugurates the new navy. More than a month earlier in October, Franklin was on the Continental Congress's committee of conference which travelled to Cambridge to review and advise Washington's rebuild of the Continental Army. On New Year's Day, a military ceremony was conducted hoisting the new American flag inaugurating the new army. Together, Morris and Franklin were the only two men to serve on *both* secret committees of congress which dealt with foreign relations and the United Colonies' pursuit of international trade networks to supply the revolutionary effort. As primary records show, both men partnered and worked with principals of the East India Company in England—one of the first successful transnational corporations of the modern era.

There have been many colorful narratives connecting the dots between the American flag and the East India Company colors, some of which we explore in Appendix B, but the seminal academic work covering this topic is Sir Charles Fawcett's 1937 paper, *The STRIPED FLAG of the EAST INDIA COMPANY, and its CONNEXION with the AMERICAN "STARS and STRIPES."*

Fawcett states:

> For the sake of completeness I have given incidents in its history after 1800, but they do not affect the main purpose of this article, which is to establish that the Company's flag was identical with the one generally known in the United States of America as "the Grand Union Flag". This was the first banner displayed in the American War of Independence to indicate a union of the thirteen States in revolt, each of which had previously used a flag of its own. [...] *On the above basis, the assertion that the*

> *Grand Union Flag was copied from the East India Company's flag has, prima facie probability.*
>
> Its striped flag had been flying for nearly two centuries, and it would at any rate be familiar to Englishmen. It seems probable that it was also well known to American seamen, who made voyages to Dutch and other European ports for various purposes, including the large traffic in smuggling tea and other heavily taxed goods into America. Thus Esek Hopkins (1718-1802), who was commissioned in December 1775 as Commander-in-Chief of the new navy of the thirteen States and on whose flagship the Grand Union Flag was first hoisted would almost certainly be acquainted with it, for not only had he been one of the leading colonial seamen, but also a privateer captain, who had made brilliant and successful ventures during the Seven Years' War (1756-63). (emphasis added)

Certainly Lt. John Paul Jones, the first man to hoist the Grand Union flag on the *Alfred*, was familiar with East India Company (EIC) ships, and most likely, their colors. Born in Scotland, Jones mentions EIC ships in 1775, "...he had suggested that if the Continental navy seized St. Helena in the mid-Atlantic, the "the vessels of the British East India Company [that dropped] anchor at that spot on their homeward trip...would inevitably fall into American hands."[1] Lt. Jones must have been struck by a tinge of irony when he had the distinction of raising the East India standard—as the "Flag of America"—for the first time on the Continental Navy's flagship, *Alfred*. Jones's later command, the *Bonhomme Richard*, was a former East Indiaman (albeit the French *Compagnie des Indes Orientales*) and was named after the protagonist of Benjamin Franklin's classic, *Poor Richard's Almanack*.

There are even more compelling reasons to associate the Grand Union flag's unveiling on the *Alfred* with the British East India Company. As mentioned, the Continental Navy's first flagship, the *Alfred*, was formally a merchantman named the *Black Prince*, built in 1774, and owned by Willing, Morris & Co.

---

[1] James C. Bradford, *John Paul Jones: And the American Navy*, (New York: Rosen, 2002), 36.

The Unsung Primary Mover: Robert Morris

The Philadelphia merchant and banking magnate, Robert Morris, was a principal of Willing, Morris & Co., and is largely an unsung primary actor in the Revolutionary War. Some of the highlights of his pivotal role in American nationhood include being one of only two men to sign all three founding scripture—the Declaration of Independence, Articles of Confederation and the U.S. Constitution. Morris was the original owner of the first two ships of the Continental Navy and provided the wharves and staging area for the outfitting of the navy's first flotilla; he procured much of the ordnance and supplies for the war effort—much of it drawn on personal credit marshaling the resources of his global trading network; only he and Benjamin Franklin sat on both secret committees of congress which conducted all foreign negotiations and supplies acquisition.

Further, he was the sole naval agent and de facto commander of the Continental Navy for much of the war (after Esek Hopkins resigned his commission); Morris personally provided the financing necessary ($16 million in today's dollars) to transport the Continental Army to Yorktown securing victory over General Cornwallis, and, hence, American victory; in the later stages of the war, Morris was responsible for floating the entire fledging colonial economy (after the continental currency crash) buoying it with his own personal credit in the form of "Morris notes." Because of this, he was honored with the sobriquet "financier of the American Revolution" and, as the Superintendent of Finance—the first executive office in American history—became the "architect" of the American free-market economy. Morris hosted George Washington at his home for the entire proceedings of the Constitutional Convention in Philadelphia; and owned the first "White House"—a Philadelphia city-house that headquartered both the Washington and Adams administrations—among numerous other pivotal contributions. He was accused of war profiteering by Thomas Paine in 1779, and after a congressional investigation, exonerated. Morris was considered the wealthiest American coming out of the war. In the 1790s, he co-owned and managed an astounding 6 million acres in America. When an international economic bubble burst with the rise of Napoleon in Europe, he went bankrupt and was thrown in debtor's prison. It is most likely

Morris's ignominious and dramatic fall that caused his critical contributions and pivotal role during the birth of our nation to have been largely overlooked by later historians.

Without Robert Morris's industry, savvy, and international connections, the outcome of the Revolutionary War may have been entirely different. His contributions, it would seem, were at least on par with the great luminary Founders and Framers we all readily recognize, Washington, the Adamses, Jefferson, Franklin, Paine, Lee, Hamilton, Henry, Madison, etc., etc. It's important to note that the ideological freedoms expressed so elegantly by Jefferson's pen were equally matched by the creation of a free-market economy not burdened by the capricious whims of the crown; two chief characteristics—ideological and economic—framing what the new nation would become, creating a clean break from Old Europe.

How Morris becomes a key figure in the Grand Union story is seen through his extensive international reach and connections to officers in the East India Company. Morris was a prototype for today's globalist, innovating a latticework of shipping lanes and trading methodologies, that, today, comprise the primary means of capital interlocution for the predominant institutions on the planet, namely, multi-national conglomerates. Morris biographer, Charles Rappleye, stated that Morris, "was a global capitalist at the very dawn of global capitalism," and was known to say things like, "commerce should be as free as the air."

Morris built on these ideas—free enterprise, free capital markets—and these concepts and memes became the foundational pillars of the American free-market economy—a crucial accompaniment to the religious, social, and ideological freedoms brought to the world by what is, today, known as one of the oldest operating constitutional democracies.

"No Men in This City Can Serve the East India Compy With More Fidelity or Advantage"

During the tea crisis in 1773, Morris's connection to the East India Company is first established by his negotiations as warden of the port of Philadelphia with the captain of the tea ship *Polly*. Morris intercedes between protesters and convinces the captain to return to England with his cargo. In Boston, this conflict resulted in an entirely different outcome via the Boston Tea Party. Benjamin Franklin, at that time acting as colonial agent in England, was alarmed by this reckless act in Boston and offered to recompense the company for its losses.

Morris's actions with regard to the Philadelphia tea incident are lauded in a letter written to Thomas Walpole, esq., of England, by Thomas Wharton in December 27, 1773.

> "I am sensible that no Men in this city [Philadelphia] can serve the East India Compy with more Fidelity or Advantage than the House of Willing and Morris of this City Merchts."[2]

The letter's recipient, Thomas Walpole, esq., and his partner, Joshua Vanneck, were heavily involved with East India Company. "During the early 1750s, the financiers Samson Gideon, Gerrard and Joshua Vanneck, and Joseph and Michael Salvador had advanced large sums to the Company…"[3] Thomas Walpole was elected director of the East India Company in 1753, "…he took an active part in the affairs of the Company."[4] Walpole was a proponent of promoting increased free trade with the colonies and opposed British policies in America. In autumn of 1775, Walpole states in the British House of Commons, "My sentiments, however, have been confirmed, not altered, by our late unsuccessful experiments in America; as I have constantly disapproved every Act for imposing taxes on the colonies."[5]

On 13 January 1776, Walpole wrote to Lord Grafton urging a more measured tone toward America. "Surely, my Lord Duke, it is exceedingly imprudent for ministers, both with respect to themselves and their country, to push things to an extremity whence it be impossible to bring them back, except by such means as must lay a foundation of division and animosity in the nation for many years to come."[6]

In 1769, Walpole partnered with Benjamin Franklin in the *Grand Ohio Company*, sometimes known as the *Vandalia Company* or the *Walpole Company*. These were land speculation deals in North America, "to buy from the Crown a large area on the borders of Virginia, recently ceded by the Six Nations."[7]

Figure 28. *"Drawn by Benjamin Franklin"—French color woodblock print, possibly created by Benjamin Franklin while in France in 1776-1777. It depicts the "Grand Union" as the first American flag.* Private Collection / Archives Charmet / Bridgeman Images.

Benjamin Franklin, living in London as a colonial agent to the Crown for the decade prior to the Revolutionary War, was absolutely familiar with the affairs of the East India Company, and as an aspiring oceanographer, philosopher, and scientist, was certainly familiar with the company's flag. In 1773—a few months before the Boston Tea Party—Franklin comments on British support for America.

> "With regard to the sentiments of the people here in general concerning America, I must say we have among them many friends and well-wishers. The dissenters are all for us, and many of the merchants and manufacturers."[8]

This hints at diverging interests between the emerging mercantile class and the old system of English peerage. When the Boston Tea Party occurred, Franklin was shocked calling it "an act of violent in-justice," and offered to raise funds or reimburse the company for the lost cargo. Upon his return to America, Franklin worked closely with Robert

Morris on many affairs of the Continental Congress including both men holding seats on the two secret committees.

Franklin defends Walpole in letter dated 27 December 1775, from Philadelphia, "I can hardly suspect Mr Walpole of the Practise against you which you mention, especially as he was then expecting to have Lands of his own in America, wherein the Productions you were about to introduce must have been beneficial."

Walpole's brother, the Hon. Richard Walpole, "was captain of an East-Indiaman until 1758 when he changed to the 'steady and profitable profession of banker'. He joined the London firm of Cliff, Walpole and Clarke, and in 1763 acted as agent for Clive and East India Company…"

Immediately following the tea incident in the colonies in 1774, Robert Morris enters into business relations with Sir Francis Baring of the Baring Bank—what was to become England's oldest merchant bank. Sir Francis Baring, 1st Baronet, not only advocated for liberalization of trade with the American colonies through the course of the war, but eventually became a director of the East India Company by 1779 and the company's chairman by 1792. The "Barings had begun to invest in the East India Company in 1776… By 1783, Francis Baring had been accepted as the leader of the City (London) interest on the Court of Directors of the East India Company."[9]

The Barings's first deal in North America was with Morris's firm in 1774. Through the course of the war, Morris was the chief supplier of the Continental Army and Navy and the Baring "family actually supplied the British forces in the field during the American War of Independence."[10] In some sense, this co-mingling of war profiteering, international trade, and nation-building by Morris and Baring could be seen as a pivotal development in the birth of the modern "military industrial complex."

Further, to fully understand the magnitude and significance of the Barings's role in the quickly maturing nation, they were actually the entity that facilitated the Louisiana Purchase by acting as the fiscal agent between Napoleon and the United States. This land acquisition doubled the size of the United States of America.

The business relations between Morris, Franklin, Walpole, and Baring reveal that at least awareness of EIC interests were in close proximity to American leaders. The fact these men were in business together makes the possibility of a real connection between the EIC and Grand Union

Figure 28. *The* Adler Von Lubeck *was the most powerful warship of its time (circa 1565) and featured red-and-white stripes on its hull and banners. It was the flagship of the "Queen of the Hanseatic League" (a.k.a. the city of Lubeck). The Hanseatic League was a vast trading network of Northern European cities that operated under Lubeck Law (circa 1226)—governance by a council of merchants as opposed to regional monarchs, dukes, or kings.* Marinemaler Olaf Rahardt: www.marinemaler-olaf-rahardt.de

flags more plausible. As mercantile interests continued to cleave apart from royal control, the EIC flag, perhaps, in some way, symbolized a new, independent economic paradigm that was emerging on the world's stage.

In fact, the red-and-white stripe convention had long been associated with merchant trade and in a way that was decidedly detached from royal control. A few decades before the formation of the East India Company, the Hanseatic League's flagship, the *Adler Von Lubeck*, sported a red-and-white striped banner in addition to her hull being adorned with horizontal red-and-white striping (Figure 28). The *Adler Von Lubeck*, or "Eagle of Lubeck," was the most powerful warship of its day with Lubeck as the capital city of a vast trading network that had dominated Northern European trade for hundreds of years. The Hanseatic League operated under the Law of Lubeck, which, in 1226, was a constitutional framework granting political power to a council of merchants, as opposed to tribal monarchs, dukes, or kings. Eventually, about 100 cities in the league adopted governments based on Lubeck Law. London was a trading partner of the Hanseatic League with the wharves and offices of *Die Hansa* located in an area known as "Steelyard."

Possibly derived from the colors of the *Adler Von Lubeck* and other Hanseatic cities like Bremen, the red-and-white stripes of the East India Company standard may have carried this propitious attitude toward the emerging reign of trade forward. It has been suggested that the stripes may have been representative of the shipping lanes throughout the trading network. Although conjecture, the independent nature of both the Hanseatic League and what would become the British East India Company would seem to suggest a level of shared interest and common philosophy that may have contributed to the EIC incorporating Hanseatic symbolism into their own designs. If so, as the striped symbolism made its journey from *Die Hansa* to the EIC and then to the American republic, it embodied a sense of a new *modus operandi*—no longer would kings be kings, but rather business was now "king." It is interesting to note that this new American economic model—based upon constitutional law and trade—was quite possibly influenced more by Lubeck Law than its contemporary cousin, the well-known *Magna Carta (1215)*.

Fawcett continues:

> The distinguished American leader, Benjamin Franklin (1706-90), was another who must have known of it [East India Company flag]. He came to London as a young man to finish his education as a printer (December 1724 to July 1726), and made two other long stays in England from 1757 to 1762 and from 1764 to 1774. During the latter period he acted as London agent for the opposition to the King's Government in four of the American colonies. In 1761 he made a trip to Holland and during his third period of residence he visited France and Germany. He thus had opportunities of seeing the Company's flag; and even if he did not himself see it, it did not need the omniscience of Macaulay's schoolboy for him and hundreds of other English settlers in America to know of it. He would naturally be interested in the East India Company, for (in addition to its prominence as a mercantile body) it was concerned in the agitation that was going on in the American colonies. Thus in a letter of 5 January 1773 Franklin mentions a report that the Company had tea and other goods to the value of four millions in its warehouses, for which it wanted a market, and says that he had remarked on the imprudence of keeping up the duty on tea, which had thrown that trade into the hands of the Dutch and

> others who smuggled it into America. On this point the Company was in agreement with Franklin, for in 1667 it had advocated an alteration of the duties to prevent smuggling, and in the beginning of 1773 it urged the abolition of the duty of 3d. a pound on tea in America, which Lord North's ministry insisted on retaining.
>
> Franklin, therefore, far from having reason to dislike the Company, could properly regard it almost as an ally. Another thing that might dispose him to favour its flag was that it symbolized independence, in the sense that the Company's administration in India was not then directly controlled by the King's ministers, for it was not till 1784 that the well-known "Board of Control" was established. Franklin was Chairman of the "Committee of Conference", consisting of himself and two others, which was appointed by the second continental congress on 15 June 1775 to confer with General Washington on the organization of the land forces. He is likely, therefore, to have had an influential voice in settling their flag.

Although mentioned in some of the Grand Union origin fables (see Appendix B), the East India tea involved in the Boston Tea Party was not transported to the colonies by East India Company ships. Therefore, as Fawcett concludes, the merchant ships involved in the incident most likely flew "the ordinary British mercantile flag, viz, the red ensign (see Figure 17). [...] It follows that the theory favoured by some English and American writers that the Company's ships were frequent visitors to American ports and its flag a familiar sight to the colonists is a pure myth."

However, there is evidence of the prominent placement of the East India Company's flag in the colonies—at least an iconographic depiction of the device.

Peter Ansoff, in his excellent sleuthing paper for the North American Vexillological Association, *A Striped Ensign in Philadelphia in 1754?*, reveals the background story on a persistent mystery in American vexillology. In 1754, an engraving of the Philadelphia waterfront included in the foreground of the image a large merchant ship flying a striped ensign with the British Union Jack in the canton. The flag strongly resembles the Grand Union flag because, as Ansoff surmises, it is the East India Company's flag from an older illustration copied over to the new engraving. The original image was from a painting of Bombay, India, made in 1732. That painting included a large East India merchant ship flying the company flag which featured thirteen red-and-white stripes and a British Union in the canton (Figure 29). As Ansoff discovers, evidently, a London engraver, in a kind of low-tech Photoshop technique, copied the illustration of this earlier ship as a mirror image when engraving the Philadelphia waterfront years later.

The 1754 engraving of the Philadelphia waterfront was the brain child of Thomas Penn, one of the sons of William Penn, the founder of Pennsylvania. It was a marketing effort to match other contemporary engravings of New York and Boston showing those ports as bustling centers of American trade and commerce.

Ansoff states that two printing runs of the pertinent Philadelphia engraving were made—one of 500 copies and another of 250. The waterfront engraving was fairly large—6 ft. 10 in. wide by nearly two feet tall—and copies were undoubtedly displayed in prominent locations in the colonies. This places the East India Company flag—in an iconographic marketing push for Philadelphia—in the colonies at least 21 years before the American Revolution.

Figure 30. *A 1732 painting (below with detail on right) of Bombay featuring a ship flying the East India Company ensign with thirteen red-and-white stripes and the British Union Jack in the canton.*

[2] Thomas Wharton, "Notes and Queries," *The Pennsylvania Magazine of History and Biography*, Volume 14, 1890, 79.

[3] H.V. Bowen, *The Business of Empire: The East India Company and Imperial Britain, 1756-1833*, (Cambridge, England: Cambridge University Press, 2008), 34.

[4] Sir Lewis Bernstein Namier, et al, ed., *The House of Commons 1754-1790*, (London: H.M.S.O, 1964), 598.

[5] Ibid. 600.

[6] Ibid.

[7] Ibid.

[8] *To Thomas Cushing, Esq.*, July 7, 1773, The private correspondence of Benjamin Franklin, comprising a series of letters on miscellaneous, litarary, and political subjects: Written between the years 1753 and 1790; illustrating the memoirs of his public and private life, and developing the secret history of his political transactions and negociations [*sic*]. Now first published from the originals, Volume 1 (Google eBook)

[9] Peter G. Zhang, *Barings Bankruptcy and Financial Derivatives*, (Singapore: World Scientific, 1996), 12

[10] Peter G. Zhang, *Barings Bankruptcy and Financial Derivatives*, (Singapore: World Scientific, 1996), 13

Summary

> If I have shown any bias in favour of the Company's flag [i.e. being connected to the American flag], I am at any rate justified in relying on one qualification that no other rival can claim, viz. the fact of its being identical with the Grand Union Flag. That this was due to mere coincidence, without the designers of the latter banner being aware of it, seems to me improbable. ~ Sir Charles Fawcett

Although no direct evidence of the two flags being connected has yet to emerge, this new circumstantial evidence helps fill out the potential for the two devices being related. The fact that Robert Morris, Benjamin Franklin and key principals within the East India Company were in business together before and after the revolution would at least seem to indicate the possibility of shared interest. The symbolism of the East India Company flag may have been seen as a desirable and transitional step toward the economic independence that made up a large portion of colonial grievances against parliament, and eventually, King George. Adopting it as the standard of united opposition to British policies may have been a subtle telegraph to the rising mercantile class on both continents. There is also the possibility that as a symbol of economic independence, the EIC flag design communicated a novel fashion sense, so-to-speak, and the red-and-white stripes, as the merchant's banner, just looked cool. These red-and-white stripes may have originated with the flag of Bremen and Lubeck, two capital cities in the Hanseatic League, which maintained a trading house, *Steelyard*, in London. The *Adler Von Lubeck*, in its day the most powerful warship in the world, featured red-and-white striping on its hull and a red-and-white striped ensign. As the flagship of *Die Hansa*—the most advanced trading network in Europe—the *Adler* may have contributed to the perception of the red-and-white stripe convention as being the "merchants' colors." It would be natural for the EIC to adopt this convention, and then later, the United Colonies, as a republic born from England but based on religious *and* economic freedoms.

Appendix B: Fables and Myths About the Grand Union

While history has to yet to provide any primary source documentation as to what drove the origin of the Grand Union flag, this hasn't prevented various authors from offering anecdotal and even myth-like narratives of how this flag came into existence—like a game of Chinese Whispers the story gets passed along from one to the next. This section provides a compilation of some of these myths and tales.

The inimitable author, systems theorist, and futurist, Buckminster Fuller, in his seminal work Critical Path (1981), relates a fanciful story of a captured East India Company flag[11] from the tea ship *Dartmouth* during the Boston Tea Party in December of 1773. Fuller erroneously states that this was the exact flag Washington used when he took command of the Continental Army in Cambridge in the summer of 1775. However, the Grand Union / EIC flag could not have been used in the summer of 1775 because its first appearance was months later on the *Alfred* on 3 December 1775.

Fuller relays an interesting narrative of how he stumbled across the EIC flag.

> "By pure chance I happened to uncover this popularly unknown episode of American history. Commissioned in the 1970 by the Indian government to design new airports in Bombay, New Delhi, and Madras, I was visiting the grand palace of the British fortress in Madras, where the English first established themselves in India in 1600. There I saw a picture of Queen Elizabeth I and the flag of the East India Company of 1600 A.D., with it's thirteen red and white horizontal stripes and its superimposed crosses in the upper corner. What astonished me was that this flag (which seemed to be the American flag) was apparently being used in 1600 A.D. 175 years before the American Revolution."[11]

Fuller offers a dubious explanation of where this flag originated.

> "In our tracing of the now completely invisible world power structures it is important to note that, while the British Empire as a world government lost the American Revolution, the power structure behind it did not lose the war. The most visible of the power-structure identities was the East India Company, and entirely private enterprise whose flag as adopted by Queen Elizabeth in 1600 happened to have thirteen red

> and white horizontal stripes with a blue rectangle in its upper left-hand corner. The blue rectangle bore in red and white the superimposed crosses of St. Andrew and St. George. When the Boston Tea Party occurred, the colonists dressed as Indians boarded the East India Company's three ships and threw overboard their entire cargoes of high-tax tea. They also took the flag from the masthead of the largest of the 'East Indiamen'—the *Dartmouth*."[12]

Fuller's history is inaccurate in several places. Firstly, the three Boston Tea Party ships—the *Dartmouth*, *Eleanor* and *Beaver*—were American vessels, not "*East Indiamen*." The American ships had only been hired to transport East India Company tea. Secondly, Fuller propagates the now disproven Betsy Ross myth about Washington seeking her out in 1776 to "repackage" the American flag by replacing the British Union with thirteen stars.

Fuller then concludes with a non-sequitur:

> "While the British government lost the 1776 war, the East India Company's owners who constituted the invisible power structure behind the British government not only did not lose but moved right into the new U.S.A economy along with the latter's most powerful landowners."[13]

Even if Fuller's story were true, there is still no explanation offered of why a flag captured by the Boston Tea Party commandoes and then later used by the Continental Army was evidence of the British "invisible power structure" moving "right into" America. In fact, the capture of the EIC flag—at least on its face—would seem to point toward an opposite conclusion. Nevertheless, it is a myth, as the American vessels involved in the tea party did not fly EIC flags. Further, for the "transference of power" theory to have substance we would need to see evidence of business dealings between leaders of both the EIC and the quickly maturing American government and economy—some of which is provided above in Appendix A.

Elements of Fuller's story were most likely drawn from a British Publication, "A Manual of Flags" by W. J. Gordon (1933) in which he refers to the Boston Tea Party ships being "East Indiamen" and while relaying the story of the Prospect Hill flag raising, mentions, "…the flag he [Washington] had hoisted was one of the tea-ship flags, all up to date, not with the cross of St. George, but with the Union that had come in 1707[…] …the flag, which is that of the East India Company in every thread of its bunting."

Figure 31. *Postcard from Somerville, MA from Jan. 1, 1976 that commemorates the 200th anniversary of the raising of the Grand Union flag.*

Gordon also reprises another oft-repeated myth concerning the Grand Union's origins misquoting an 1890 publication "Our Flag; or, the Evolution of the Stars and Stripes, etc." by Robert Allen Campbell. Gordon states the exact time and place when the Grand Union flag was decided upon—after an inspiring speech offered by Benjamin Franklin at a dinner party on 13 December 1775 which was also attended by Washington. However, the original Campbell story depicts the speech being made by a mysterious figure called the "Professor,"—not Franklin.

This mysterious figure is most likely drawn from a fictionalized romance written in 1847 by George Lippard entitled, "*Washington and his Generals: or, Legends of the Revolution.*" Lippard offers a transcription of "The Speech of the Unknown"—a persuasive and passionate soliloquy by a mysterious figure during the Continental Congress's critical debate concerning the Declaration of Independence. Famed esoteric compiler, Manley P. Hall's "Secret Destiny of America" also reprises this tale about an "unknown speaker" or "mysterious professor."

The last interesting Grand Union / EIC flag myth is from a political book by progressive talk show host Thom Hartmann. In Hartmann's *Unequal Protection* (2010), he conflates the various corporate charters granted to the Virginia Company and the East India Company mentioning that the "companies had interlocking boards, as Sir Thomas Smythe administered the America operations of both from his house." Hartmann

Figure 32. *U.S. postage stamp.* United States Postal Service.

states the, "company's influence was pervasive wherever it went," and concerning the thirteen red-and-white stripes of the EIC flag, he writes, "many historians believe it was because most of the stockholders in the East India Company were initiates in the Masonic Order, and the Masons considered thirteen to be a metaphysically powerful number. Virtually every signer of the Constitution was also a Mason, which may be why they chose to limit the original colonies to thirteen. But that's all speculation; nobody knows for sure, or, if they do, they're not telling."

Hartmann's last sentence stands on its own regarding most of the "facts" his story. First, there are documented versions of the EIC flag ranging from 9 to 15 stripes, so the 13 striped version is not necessarily an outstanding specimen. Additionally, of the 39 signers of the U.S. Constitution only one-third were known Freemasons.

---

[11] In December 1773, men disguised as either Mohawk or Narragansett Indians armed with small hatchets and clubs boarded East India Ships and dumped two thousand crates of recently shipped tea into the harbor. Adjusting for inflation, the value of the cargo was nearly $2 million dollars. The actions of these men sparked an international incident that lead to Concord/ Lexington in 1775 and the beginning of the American Revolutionary War of Independence in 1776.

[12] R. Buckminster Fuller, Critical Path, (New York: St. Martin's, 1981), 78

[13] Ibid. 77-78.

Acknowledgements

This work would not have been possible without the selfless contributions of many. This includes librarians and archivists at numerous collections, universities, and historical societies; owners of copywritten material that have granted licenses for inclusion in this work; numerous colleagues and experts; and most importantly, my family and friends—you know who you are. Here is a short and no doubt incomplete list of those who pressed in to make this publication a reality…

Architect of the Capitol

Archives Charmet / Bridgeman Images

Tom and LaDonna Appelbaum

Alison Barnes Martin

John L. Bell, *Boston 1775*

Jerry M. Bloomer, R.W. Norton Art Gallery

Colonial Williamsburg Foundation

Creative Commons

Jim Crossman

Hon. Joseph A. Curtatone, *Mayor of Somerville*

John De Herrera

Gillian De Lear

The Flag Institute

The Flag Research Center
Dr. Whitney Smith
Hugh L. Brady
Dr. Scot M. Guenter
Charles A. Spain

The Grand Lodge of Missouri

Dr. John B. Hattendorf, *Ernest J. King Professor Emeritus of Maritime History at the U.S. Naval War College*

Jonathan Lehmann, *Cambium Creative*

The Library of Congress
Elizabeth L. Brown, Reference Specialist
Bruce Kirby, Manuscript Reference Librarian

Brad Meltzer

Missouri Lodge of Research

National Archives and Records Administration

National Galleries of Scotland

National Portrait Gallery of the Smithsonian Institution

Navy Art Collection, Naval History and Heritage Command, United States Navy
Gale Munro, Head Curator

Massachusetts Historical Society

The New York Public Library Astor, Lenox, and Tilden Foundations

New-York Historical Society
Mariam Touba,
Edward F. O'Reilly

North American Vexillological Association–Association nord-américaine de vexillologie
Peter A. Ansoff
James J. Ferrigan, 3d
John M. Hartvigsen
Edward B. Kaye
Dr. Kenneth W. Reynolds
Gustavo Tracchia

Olaf Rahardt

Oswego County Today
Steve Yablonski, Editor-in-Chief

Michael Parker

Pennsylvania Capitol Preservation Committee

Matt Pidgeon

Douglas Rowe

Dave Rutherford, *House of Motion*

Mark Sappenfield, *Christian Science Monitor*

Somerville Historical Society
Brandon Wilson

Somerville Museum

Duane Streufert, *U.S. Flag Depot*

Brothers at *Tuscan Lodge No. 360, Ancient Free & Accepted Masons*

Tyron Palace

United States Postal Service

Kenneth Warren

Wikipedia & Wikimedia Foundation

Col. Lawrence A. Willwerth, Quartermaster, *Ancient and Honorable Artillery Company of Massachusetts*

Index

About the Author

Byron DeLear is an author, enviro-entrepreneur, media producer, and twice former U.S. House candidate. DeLear is a member of the Organization of American Historians, the Missouri Lodge of Research, and is past Editor-In-Chief for *NAVA News*, the newsletter of the North American Vexillological Association–Association nord-américaine de vexillologie. His articles and interviews have appeared in many major media outlets including NBC News, the *Christian Science Monitor*, and the *Los Angeles Times*. DeLear is co-founder of Energy Equity Funding, LLC and Managing Director and Central Regional Executive—Midwest for Ygrene Energy Fund, Inc. He keeps his finger on the pulse of a wide range of future-focused projects, and serves on boards of various non-governmental organizations and non-profits. He may be reached at: *ByronDeLear@gmail.com*

Photo: Alison Barnes Martin

Cover artwork of the Grand Union flag was illustrated by Douglas Rowe. He can be reached at: *drowe@charter.net*